ASPECTS OF WAKEFIELD 3

Aspects of
WAKEFIELD
Discovering Local History
3

Edited by
Kate Taylor

Series Editor
Brian Elliott

Wharncliffe Books

First Published in 2001 by
Wharncliffe Books
an imprint of
Pen and Sword Books Limited,
47 Church Street, Barnsley,
South Yorkshire. S70 2AS

For up-to-date information on other titles produced under the
Wharncliffe imprint, please telephone or write to:

> **Wharncliffe Books**
> **FREEPOST**
> **47 Church Street**
> **Barnsley**
> **South Yorkshire S70 2BR**
> **Telephone (24 hours): 01226 - 734555**

ISBN: 1-903425-06-9

A CIP catalogue record of this book is available from the
British Library

Cover illustration: Looking towards Marygate from the Bull Ring, by Louisa Fennell
Courtesy of Wakefield Art Gallery

Printed in the United Kingdom by
CPI UK

CONTENTS

Introduction

by

Kate Taylor

The *Aspects* series, founded in 1993, is now very well established and geographically widespread. The first *Aspects of Wakefield* was published in 1998 and was followed by a second collection of essays in 1999. Contributors to this third volume include six whose work has appeared in the earlier Wakefield books but there are also essays by four 'newcomers', reflecting their specialist research fields of golf, transport, women's history, and Wrenthorpe.

Whilst the essays are again very varied in their focus, the theme of leisure happens to link a number of them. John Goodchild takes us back to the origins of the Badsworth Hunt; David Scriven surveys a wide range of leisure activities in Ossett in the Victorian period; Brian Wallis chronicles the development of Ossett Golf Club in the early twentieth century; the Victorians' enthusiasm for 'rational recreation' – for encouraging the working class to spend their modest free time in the pursuit of knowledge – is reflected in my own essay on the Wakefield Church Institution; Coopers' bus company, recollected by J D Clayton, routinely took coalminers to work, but also provided the transport for many holiday excursions by local groups.

The men held during the First World War at Lofthouse Park must have had ample leisure! In the first *Aspects of Wakefield* we published Peter Wood's account of the creation of the Park as a commercial enterprise, with its recreational facilities. Here he shows how the Park became the home of a remarkable college for its German inmates when it became a camp for internees.

An impressive number of medieval deeds in his unique archive collection has enabled John Goodchild to undertake a study of three adjoining townships, Chevet, Sandal and Walton, in this period, characterising the landowning and settlement patterns and bringing out even something of the personalities and way of life of the inhabitants, thus providing rare insights.

The Victorian period is further represented here. Ann Barnes's account of Wakefield's many yards gives emphasis to their unwholesome condition in the early 1850s. It was the state then of the burial grounds and the threat of cholera that led to the opening of the Wakefield borough cemetery which is the subject of Anthony Petyt's essay where he includes a section on some of those interred there in the latter half of the nineteenth century. Edward Green portrays the life and obsession of Victorian eccentric Daniel Milton who laid claim – on the grounds of being the Christian Israelites' leader – to Melbourne House at Wrenthorpe.

John Goodchild's notes on brewing in Wakefield reveal the development of the industry again primarily in Victorian times. Analysis of the 1851 census has enabled Deborah Scriven to identify the pattern of employment of women in Ossett in the mid-nineteenth century.

I am grateful to each of these contributors for submitting the fruits of their scholarship. But thanks are due also to Brian Elliott, the general editor of the series and to all the staff of Wharncliffe Books.

1. CHEAPER BY THE YARD: WAKEFIELD YARDS

by Ann Barnes

YARDS ARE A FAMILIAR SIGHT in many towns and cities. The streets are lined with diverse buildings interspersed with archways leading into yards crammed with buildings, often haphazardly arranged (Figures 1-3). This has its origins in a system which dates back to, at the very least, early medieval times. Town streets were lined with 'croft and toft' holdings – long, narrow plots with, originally, a homestead for the occupier and his family and a 'garden' or small-holding plot growing food for the family – vegetables, possibly fruit, hens, even a pig which could be fed, in part at least, on household, garden or scavenged waste, perhaps a cow or goat for milk, butter and cheese. These latter were highly negotiable products, at a time when subsistence economy was the prevalent system and food was mainly for domestic consumption or for trade. As the social and economic climate changed, a more recognisably modern system took over and many families ran some sort of business, based in or around the plot, and capitalising on the skills and expertise of the family or its individuals.

Figure 1. The entrance to a yard off Westgate in 2001.

Figure 2. Scott's Yard. Westgate, as drawn by Henry Clarke in the early 1890s.

Over the years assorted outhouses might be added, built onto the back of the dwelling – extra rooms for domestic purposes, for privies, for storage, for stabling and for workshops. At some point it became apparent that it would be more lucrative to turn the land over to the provision of further dwellings; and in the days long before the advent of town planning large numbers of families could be accommodated

Figure 3. The arched entrance to White Horse Yard, Westgate, in 2001.

Figure 4. Library Yard, Northgate.
The John Goodchild Collection.

Figure 5. A corner in Library Yard.
The John Goodchild Collection.

in dwellings squeezed into the long narrow plot (Figures 4-5). When adjacent plots had undergone the same process the typical appearance of yards, which is still, just about, visible today, had emerged. The yards were almost always 'dead ends'; there was only rarely an exit at the bottom or far end.

As towns developed and yards proliferated – virtually every building which fronted the main street could spawn a yard – names were necessarily coined to distinguish and identify the yards. When that yard developed behind or beside a public house it would probably take its name from that hostelry; examples of this type of naming abound in Wakefield, as in most other towns and cities (Figure 6). Other yards took their name from the owner (or occupier)

Figure 6. Old Crown Yard. *The John Goodchild Collection.*

Figure 7. Dispensary Yard, Northgate, as drawn by Henry Clarke in the 1890s.

of the dwelling or business which fronted the street, or occasionally from some other person of significance associated with the yard, from an important building, institution or function located there, or from some other aspect of its situation (Figure 7).

In Wakefield the largest numbers of yards are located, predictably, in Kirkgate, Westgate, and Northgate, the three main ancient routes into and out of the town, where the burgage plots were originally located (Figure 8). A few yards were scattered around the other town-centre (or from 1888 city-centre) streets and the other main route out of town, that now known as Stanley Road, but formerly the Wakefield/Aberford turnpike road.

Figure 8. Ordnance Survey map of c1888 showing some of the yards off Northgate.

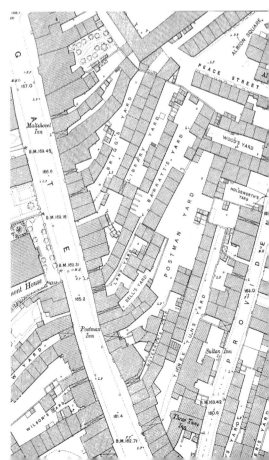

All maps of Wakefield so far known share the same shortcoming: they illustrate many more yards than they name. Walker's 1823 map of Wakefield shows a substantial number of yards together with their names; the c1851 sixty inches to the mile Ordnance Survey map of Wakefield and the c1888 ten feet to the mile OS map are quite helpful; there is an excellent and detailed series of maps dating from 1913-14 , but although many yards are shown hardly any are named. Registers of Electors and Burgess Rolls for Wakefield, from

YARD NAME	1832	1835	1837
BULL		2 houses	4 house & c
CHURCH		House	
COCK & SWAN	House	Warehouse	Warehouse
FLEECE	House & shop		
LITTLE BULL			Malt kiln
OLD CHURCH			House
OLD CROWN	House & shop	House	2 houses
OXLEY'S	House	House	2 houses
PLAYHOUSE	Warehouse		
POSTMAN'S		House & stable	House & stable
RED LION	2 houses	House	House
ROBSON'S	House & stable	House	House
RODNEY	House	3 Houses	3 Houses & c
SAW	4 Houses	House, house shop	House
SMALLPAGE	Brewery		
STAR		Warehouse	2 warehouses
TALBOT & FALCON	House & stable	House & stable	House & stable
THOMPSONS		House	House
WHITE HORSE	Warehouse, house	House, 2 warehouses	Warehouse
WHITE SWAN	House	House, kiln	House, house & shop
WHITE'S		3 houses	House
WINDMILL	House & shop		
WOOLPACK'S		House, 2 warehouses	3 houses, 2 with w/h
TOTAL PREMISES	**18**	**27**	**29**

Figure 9. The Registers of Electors and Burgess Rolls show something of the development of the yard system. Between 1832 and 1837 the number of properties located in yards, whose owners or occupiers had acquired a vote increased markedly.

1832, survive, in the Local Studies Department at Balne Lane Library, as do the Year Books produced by the Borough of Wakefield for the use of members of the council and from 1872 until 1965 most editions contained a list of all streets (including yards) within Wakefield together with their location (Figure 9). The late Joe Clay produced, in the 1970s, a schematic plan depicting the location of some Wakefield yards, apparently using the 1823 and 1851 maps, mentioned above, as his source. The street names occurring in the Wakefield censuses for 1851, 1881 and 1891 have been indexed. All these sources have been used to compile as comprehensive a list of all the yards as has been possible and, wherever feasible, their location. This is provided as an appendix (see pages 179-184).

It quickly became apparent that there were far more yard names than yards!

Some yards have changed their names, possibly more than once, some have changed their spelling, one or two names appear to have been corrupted. Just to add to the confusion sometimes two or even three different yards have the same name.

I have listed virtually every yard that I have managed to locate, excluding only those uncorroborated names and obvious misprints such as Barnsley Yd, Doncaster Yd and Hatfeild Yd, where almost certainly an error in transcription or type-setting had substituted Yd for Rd. There are many other inconsistencies, variations and corruptions of names – Tidgewell's Yard, given in several sources is assuredly a mistake for Tidswells – located on the northern side of Westgate just above Brooksbank. Spawforth Yard, also on Westgate, has been variously rendered as Spawford and Spofforth. In the Northgate/Market Place/Bull Ring area there are, in addition to the Strafford Arms Yard, Stafford, Strafford, and even on one occasion, Strafforth Yards which have so far

Figure 10. Three Tuns Yard.
The John Goodchild Collection.

proved indistinguishable, although the existence of a Strafford House in that vicinity probably gave its name to the nearby yard – however it is clear that there was a yard by one of these names further up Northgate and completely separate from the Strafford Arms Yard. By 1911 the council minutes have references to Strafford Arms Mews! I am convinced that the Three Bells Yard quoted on only one occasion, on Northgate, is in fact a careless error for the Three Tuns (Figure 10).

The name Elwick Yard appears in the 1853 trade directory; apparently the yard had been known as Wright and Elwick's in the years before 1820, the name being that of a furniture manufactory located there; Richard Wright and Edward Elwick were in partnership there between 1747 and 1771, producing furniture of the very highest quality. Many fine pieces were supplied to the Marquess of Rockingham for his Wentworth Woodhouse mansion near Rotherham. Much of their work was based on the designs produced by Thomas Chippendale in his *Gentleman and Cabinet Makers' Directory*, published in 1754 and 1762; they favoured the use of fine and rare timbers. In the summer of 2000 a few pieces were auctioned by Christie's in London and realised far in excess of the expected price of around £330,000. After the death of Wright the name was shortened. Later still the name was changed to Gill's Yard,

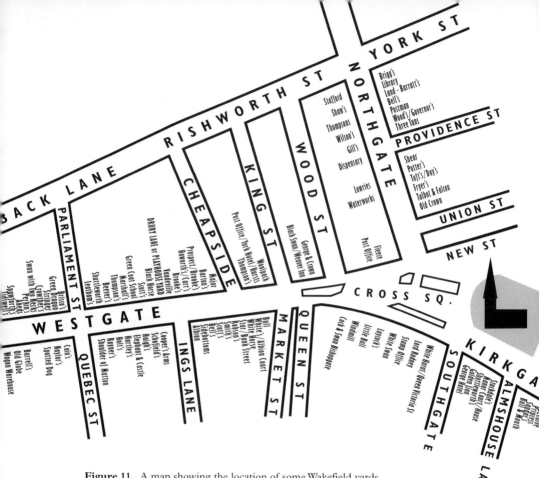

Figure 11. A map showing the location of some Wakefield yards.

a name which it retains today. In the 1857 directory an 'Errick' Yard is given with a location at the 'top of Wood Street' ;no other evidence of an Errick Yard has been found so I believe that this may have been a transcription error for Elwick; the location Elwick and Robinson's Yard occurs in the Northgate Ward Burgess Rolls for the same era, as does Robinson's Yard, the latter continuing to appear for many years.

The Playhouse Yard was to become Drury Lane. The Vaudeville and the Theatre Yards, both to be found on Westgate immediately to the east of (above) the theatre are undoubtedly the same.

Fenton Heald's Yard and Heald's Yard both appear on Kirkgate, and for a long time I suspected that they were one and the same, but it is clear from the 1887 directory that they are almost at opposite ends of Kirkgate. I believe that Shillett's and Shillito's on Northgate are the same. Major Burton's and Burton's Yards, on Westgate are probably the same but later evolved into Carter Street. On Kirkgate

Mellard's and Mellor's are almost certainly the same. On the 1823 map there are shown, unmistakably, two Brook's Yards on the north side of Westgate, one immediately above, and one immediately below Carr's Yard, but no other source has been found to confirm this (Figures 11 and 12).

Old, as a prefix to yard names, seems to be added or dropped in a totally cavalier manner: in some trade directories the Old Church Yard and the Church Yard are both used within the same volume, but I have found no other evidence to support the suggestion that these are actually different yards. The Old Green Dragon, the Green Dragon and the Dragon are, without doubt, the same, as are the Library and Old Library, the Great Bull and the Bull or even the Old Bull, the Spotted Leopard and the Leopard, the Rodney and the Lord Rodney (Figure 13). On (Upper) Kirkgate a yard appears which changes between Prince's and Princess. Some yards taking their names from adjacent public houses gain or lose the Inn in their name in a totally random way: the *Saw* (Inn), the (Old) *Globe* (Inn), the *Postman* (Inn), etc.

Fox's, or Foxes, Yard was the previous name of the (Lord) Rodney Yard and is recorded as such at the time of the sale of land on which Zion Chapel was built. The nearby Windmill Yard took its name – either directly or via the *Windmill Inn*, – from the windmill located

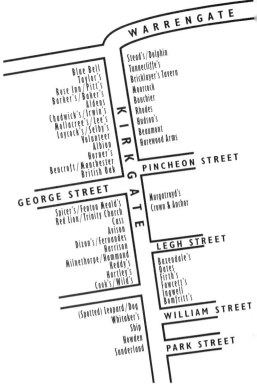

Figure 12. A map showing the location of some Wakefield yards.

Figure 13. Rodney Yard.
Collection of Peter Wood.

nearby. This was the work of John Smeaton (1724-94), the eminent civil engineer from Austhorpe near Leeds, who was probably best known for his novel design for the third Eddystone lighthouse. A drawing of the windmill survives and has been published but the person in possession of the photocopy which I have seen could not recall the source from which he had obtained it!

The 1823 map, by Walker, shows the Post Office Yard between the Market Place (Bull Ring) and Wood Street, where Radcliffe Place is now and, indeed, has been since about 1888 (it probably takes its name from the Radcliffe Printing Works then located there); the 1851 map shows the yard but gives it no name, nor do any other sources name that yard until it becomes Radcliffe Place (Figure 14). By 1851 the Post Office and its Yard have moved further down Westgate.

There is a *Fleece* on Brook Street, but another *Fleece* is listed in the Market Place (the former name of the Bull Ring) and, on a different occasion, one on Westgate; I have, so far, been unable to confirm my belief that these latter two are the same, Westgate does occasionally seem to be used to describe, not only the area now known as Westgate, but the street which links Westgate, as we understand it, to the (now) Bull Ring). The *Swan* appears to refer to the *Swan with Two Necks* and NOT the *White Swan* or the *Black Swan*; I have confirmed this, beyond doubt, by comparing it with records of different years and in different sources. However the *New Elephant*, sometimes located in the Corn Market and sometimes on New Street, is definitely not connected with the *Elephant and Castle*; the *Talbot* is on Westgate and therefore unconnected with the *Talbot and Falcon*. The (Old) Red Lion Yard leads to Trinity Church Gate and is, therefore, also known, sometimes, as Trinity Church Yard.

One or two of the trade directories list individuals and yards with just a number and street, thus: Fred Bloggs, yard 3 Blank Street.

I have assumed that this meant that Fred Bloggs was located in/at a yard adjacent to number 3 Blank Street, for which the writer had no name immediately to hand. Quite a few of these references were later identified as yards with established names, but a few remain intractable and are therefore listed just as 'yard' with the address.

Where a street number is given for the location of a yard this is, of course, approximate. Yards do not have street numbers; the number is that of one of the adjacent buildings. Sometimes it has been impossible to determine the exact location and two widely different numbers are given, meaning that the yard is somewhere between the two. The numbers are those following the massive renumbering of Wakefield streets which took place sometime between 1888 and

Figure 14. Radcliffe Place runs parallel to Wood Street diagonally across the centre of the photograph. *Wakefield Historical Publications.*

1892, and which are, generally speaking, those which are still in use today.

Wherever possible the date given in any column is that of the earliest occurrence of a yard name. The columns refer to the Wakefield Borough Yearbooks, already mentioned, the Burgess Rolls or Registers of Electors, the trade directories and maps.

On the subject of Burgess Rolls and Registers of Electors I have found that there was a surprisingly large difference between the two in terms of the numbers of people entitled to vote, the Burgess Rolls sometimes having three or four times the electorate; for example in 1850-51 the Register of Electors names fifty-eight voters living in yards, the Burgess Roll names two hundred and ten.

Some of the earlier trade directories list the Manor Court Yard as being between Westgate and Kirkgate; now this yard was located opposite the lower end of the Cathedral - about where Boots is now. The section between this point and Southgate (the upper entrance to the Ridings) is now regarded as part of (Upper) Kirkgate, but historically this, as well as Little Westgate, appear to have all formed one continuous street – Westgate. This shift between Kirkgate and Westgate may have led to a duplication of records, a yard listed in Kirkgate in one source and Westgate in another may appear twice in my listing, and although I have tried to be aware of this possibility and eliminate it from my data base, I would still rather list a yard twice than risk omitting a particular yard altogether.

The earliest readily-available source, the Baines directory of 1822, lists only a small number of yards:

BLACK SWAN	SAW
BULL	SHACKLETONS
CHURCH	SMITHS
COCK AND SWAN	STAR
FLEECE	STOTTS
LAYCOCKS	THOMPSONS
OLD CROWN	WHITE HORSE
PLAYHOUSE	WHITE SWAN
POST OFFICE	WOOLPACKS
RODNEY	

The three maps which have proved most useful in determining the exact location of a number of yards are the 1823 Walker's, and the OS maps of 1851 and 1888, even these, however, show wide divergence in the names of yards which are given.

The heyday of the yard seems to have been the late nineteenth and early twentieth centuries; the 1822 directory lists only nineteen yards, the 1830 directory lists thirty-four - the same number as the 1847 directory, but by the time of the 1887 directory a hundred and four yards are given and in the 1890-91 Burgess Roll a hundred and forty-eight different yards are named. The 1923-24 Yearbook lists a hundred and fifty-three yards, the 1927-28 lists a hundred and forty-seven, but ten years later more than twenty yards have gone, victims of the slum clearance that started in the 1930s, which was interrupted by World War Two. Many more went in the 'sanitization' and 'modernisation' of the city that occurred, in the name of progress, in the late 1950s and early 1960s.

However, by the middle of the nineteenth century outbreaks of cholera and other infectious diseases had drawn attention to the poor sanitary conditions in parts of Wakefield - the conditions in the area around Nelson Street and a number of yards gave rise to particular concern In the Report prepared by William Ranger following the inquiry which opened at the Court House in Wakefield on 21 May, 1851, and published at the end of that year, it is stated that:

> *The Cock and Swan yard was in the hands of private owners. It was a very unhealthy locality, and small-pox was then prevalent in it.*

Statements from three Wakefield doctors include the assertion that:

> *...it is especially worthy of notice how enormously in excess is the mortality of New Street, Nelson Street and of some other courts and yards, as compared with the rest of the locality, these places being... the most wanting in all sanitary appliances and arrangements.*

Ranger quotes the results of a Mr Milner's investigations:

> *It appears that out of 164 streets, lanes and yards, examined by him, in 1847, the pavements of 34 were 'good', 54 'middling' and 80, or about one half, were 'bad'. The estimated number of persons living in the badly paved streets and yards was about 6,500,*

and again from the same source:

> *Out of 168 lanes, yards and streets examined, the ventilation of 22 was 'good', 31 'middling' and 115 'bad', the former term being used where the street or yard was open at both ends, the second when one end was partially, and the third when it was entirely closed.*

from which he calculates that 2,500 persons lived in areas where the ventilation was 'middling' and almost 9,000 where it was 'bad'. E

Walker, surgeon and Medical Officer to the Union [Workhouse, etc] commented:

That there was a general want of ventilation, the houses being frequently situated in close yards, surrounded on every side and approached only by a covered archway. The cases he had attended professionally were very frequently in localities of this description.

Another report, from the Sanitary Committee, in May 1850, again quoted in Ranger:

In Providence street and several of the yards near it, the privies require cleansing of the accumulations of offensive matter. The Committee think that the state of these places might be much improved by closing up the open spaces behind them... In this street there are some most wretched and filthy places... In two of them only a few yards square, the Visiting Committee ascertained that sometimes as many as 100 persons were crammed for the night.

The Committee made similar observations when they went on a tour of inspection of parts of Wakefield:

They went through Providence Street; and in several of the yards the privies required cleansing of the accumulation of offensive matter. ...Behind the premises of Mr Harrop, in New Street there is a mass of nuisance of the very worst description. There are a number of piggeries, and a 'sump-hole for the manure, the whole of which require immediate removal. The Visiting Committee also went into Cain's yard and found a drain in an offensive state. ...In Kirkgate, behind the Parrot beer-house, the premises were in a mostly filthy state; the yard opens into Brewery street and appears to be the depot not only for filth, but also for the harbouring of improper characters.

Some piggeries, belonging to a person named Walsh at the bottom of White Swan Yard, and some privies at the top of the Cock and Swan Yard are the subject of adverse comment by the Committee. And:

[where] *the most densely crowded houses are situated, there is no scavenging* [collection of night soil] *whatever.*

The same source goes on to estimate that of 13,074 people living in yards and courts only 650 were in well-drained localities, and that nearly 12,500 existed where there was either partial drainage or no drainage at all. And that

...cellars of the houses were damp, either from the absence or defective

nature of the sewerage

The consequences of which were

That epidemics invariably haunt the same localities... in places presenting one or more of such defects as overcrowding, dampness, filth, want of ventilation, and atmospheric pollution, proximity to pigsties, offensive sewers, &c, and in narrow and confined situations badly supplied with water, and impregnated with organic matters from filthy streets, cesspools, inefficient drainage, and the like.

W R Milner gave evidence to Ranger and his Committee that

...a yard in Kirkgate, containing about eight houses; the nightsoil from the adjoining yard oozed through the wall of one of the houses in this place, and the health of the occupants had been affected in consequence; they complained also of the offensive smell caused by this nuisance.

On the provision of so-called clean water -

There are no public stand-cocks or fountains. There are about 200 service-cocks for the supply of the poor people living near them.

...very general concurrence of the medical men as to the scanty supply of water to the poorer quarter of the town... but one standpipe is provided for a number of dwellings.

The want of water is more particularly noticed in the unhealthy localities of... Nelson Street, Cock and Swan yard... which have been, and still are, in a greater or lesser degree, the seats of fever and pestilence (Figure 15).

Charles Morton, Inspector of Coal Mines is scathing about the quality of water supplied:

Not only is the source unwholesome, but that means used to purify the

Figure 15. Table drawn up by W R Milner in 1851 showing the condition of the ventilation etc of Wakefield's lanes, yards and streets.

District.	No. of yards, &c. examined in each district.	Ventilation of yards and streets.			Drainage.			Paving.			Number of privies.	Covered cesspools.	Open cesspools.	Stagnant water.	Dungheaps.	Stable and cowhouses.	Pigsties.	Other nuisances.	Number of houses.	Estimated population at 4·72 per house.
		Good.	Middling.	Bad.	Good.	Middling.	Bad.	Good.	Middling.	Bad.										
Westgate, South	33	7	7	19	-	5	28	10	8	15	125	9	83	8	16	48	56	3	357	1,685
Westgate, North	28	2	5	21	-	1	27	-	13	15	73	6	47	7	9	46	16	-	449	2,119
Northgate, West	10	1	2	7	1	2	7	1	8	1	20	3	9	2	6	1	-	-	291	1,374
Northgate, East	18	-	5	13	1	3	14	6	5	7	89	9	76	8	27	48	41	9	467	2,204
Wrengate, North	8	-	3	5	-	-	8	1	1	6	15	2	10	2	2	5	5	1	96	453
Wrengate, South	5	1	1	3	-	-	5	1	1	3	17	7	8	4	2	5	15	-	60	283
Kirkgate, West	33	4	3	26	3	3	27	3	13	17	71	5	65	8	5	12	40	-	371	1,751
Kirkgate, East	28	3	4	21	3	2	23	8	5	15	53	2	36	9	5	9	16	2	294	1,388
Primrose Hill	5	4	1	-	-	-	5	4	-	1	53	-	36	-	1	-	52	1	322	1,520
Totals	168	22	31	115	8	16	144	34	54	80	516	43	370	48	43	174	241	16	2,707	13,074

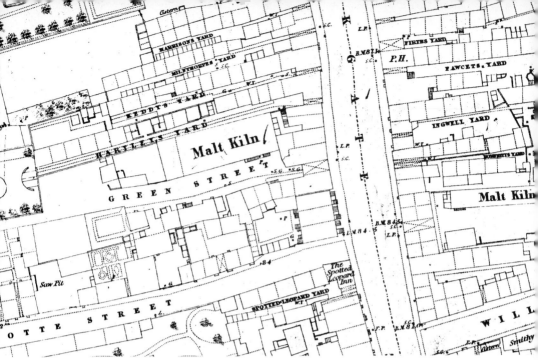

Figure 16. Ordnance Survey map c1851 showing some of the yards off Kirkgate.

water are imperfect, and the price charged by the Company in excess of what it ought to be.

L Hamerton, a resident ratepayer complained

That the inhabitants were subjected to considerable inconvenience, from being obliged to lay the water-pipes up the yards, which frequently contained a number of dwelling-houses belonging to different owners.

Time and time again it is asserted, in the Report, that it would be cheaper to provide adequate sanitary arrangements for the poorer areas of the town, than to suffer the consequences of the repeated epidemics. 'The cost of a cholera visitation for one year will more than cover the cost of a drain.'

The Chief Constable reported to the Sanitary Committee in June 1850, and he reiterates many of the complaints already quoted, and

In Wrengate are some nuisances; but the most offensive were in Bolland's Yards, two close and confined yards; the inhabitants of one of them complained very much of bad smells and its unhealthy state. ....there still appears room for very extensive improvements, especially in the following places to which the attention of the Committee is particularly called, namely, Fawcett's Yard, Ingwell Yard, Brewery Street, Jaques Yard and Blue Bell Yard. Bakehouse Yard which was formerly in a very filthy state, is much improved; but there are four

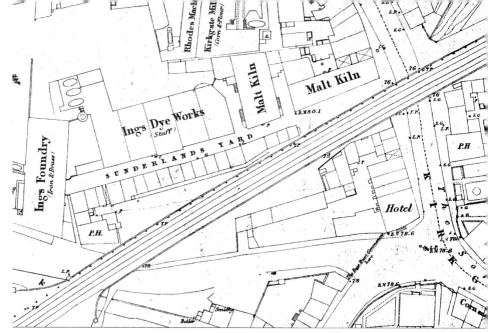

Figure 17. Ordnance Survey map c1851 showing Sunderland's Yard, Kirkgate.

privies in this yard, which are used by a very large number of the inhabitants, and which might, with a trifling expense, be very much remedied.

Walsh and his piggeries are again mentioned, apparently his occupation was collecting pig manure, to supply the clothiers of Ossett, and elsewhere;

and that at different places throughout the borough, there are accumulations of it kept for the purpose of sale to Walsh, which becomes very offensive to the inhabitants in the different neighbourhoods, and especially so in hot weather.

Samuel Dennison stated

That he had, on and off, acted as a scavenger for the last twenty years. ... He only removed the soil when he could find a purchaser for it. In one yard, occupied by 360 people, the owner of the property removed the refuse himself. In this yard, the pits, were in some cases, two yards square and three yards deep; these were cleansed four times in a year.

At this time there were stated to be 64 cow-houses and 462 pigsties within the Borough of Wakefield. Many of these, by the very nature of the town, must have been situated in yards.

Dr Netten Radcliffe had been asked to report on the sanitary conditions of Wakefield, with particular attention to the conditions that had given rise to complaints about the insanitary state of certain localities, including Eastmoor, Westgate Common and the yards in

Kirkgate particularly Hartley's and Sunderland Yards, and Talbot [and Falcon] Yard (Figures 16 and 17). His report, published in 1869, includes such graphic and detailed description of some of the yards in Wakefield that I make no apology for quoting from his report at length. Speaking of Eastmoor he referred to:

> *Ill-constructed and ill-arranged cottages originally, and ill-tended subsequently, have deteriorated so as to become in too many instances hardly fit for human residences; privies and middensteads worse constructed and worse placed are saturated with their excrementatious contents and give off incessantly offensive and noxious effluvia; and an imperfectly drained and imperfectly protected surface is sodden with filth. I would especially instance the state of the cottages, privies, middensteads, paving and surface drainage of Camplin's Yard, where, I may add, there is but one water stand-pipe for twenty inhabited houses, and from that pipe the water flowed slowly at the time of my inspection of the yard.*

Of Westgate Common he wrote

> *The description I have given of the cottages on Eastmoor applies equally to those on Westgate Common... At the west extremity of Westgate, within the limits of the Common, are two adjoining courts known as Boiler Yard and Marriott's Yard.*
>
> *The cottages in the former are old, in the latter new. Boiler Yard was the scene of a severe outbreak of typhoid fever in 1868. The yard is a quadrangle, entirely shut in excepting a narrow passage communicating with the street. It contains seven cottages, and in six of these there were cases of fever. Traversing the yard from right to left, and taking the cottages in the order in which they come, there were two cases of fever in the first; one case in the second; three cases, of which one died, in the third; two cases, one fatal, in the fourth; two in the fifth; and three in the sixth, making totals of thirteen cases and two deaths in the six cottages. A privy and midden are on the east side of the yard adjoining the fourth cottage; and nearer to the north-west angle of the yard than the centre, is the grated opening of a drain, apparently untrapped. The arrangement of the yard is radically vicious, and eminently adapted to foster infectious disease; but its worst faults have been permitted to be repeated in the newer buildings adjoining, which enter into the formation of Marriott's Yard. The cottages in this yard, ten in number, placed five on each side, are much loftier than in Boiler Yard. They form a confined yard, which is approached by an archway from the street, and is closed at the*

opposite extremity by the backs of houses of equal height. The privies and middensteads are placed at the end of one of the rows of cottages, in a position least apt to give rise to nuisance. Some of the cottages are double and placed back to back, and none have through ventilation. Narrow, closed courts, approached by covered passages are a marked peculiarity in the arrangement of the older parts of Wakefield, and it would appear that this most objectionable disposition is permitted to be carried out in some of the newer buildings.

Of the yards off Kirkgate he wrote:

The peculiarity in the arrangement of houses referred to at the close of the preceding section is particularly marked in Kirkgate. It is rare, perhaps, to see a street of such length, and having so large a number of inhabited courtyards in the rear communicating with it, in which the number of breaks in the line of houses on both sides is so few. The courtyards are, for the most, part, entered by passages which traverse the houses fronting to the street.

Hartley's Yard is a courtyard so approached. It is a long narrow space, closed at the further extremity, and having no opening for communication but the passage to the street. It is shut in, in front of the houses within it, by the backs of buildings and by a high wall which separates it from an adjoining yard. At the end near the street, Hartley's Yard is about twelve feet wide, at the further end about ten feet. Six cottages open into the latter part of the yard. These cottages have windows only toward the yard. Two were unoccupied at the time of my visit. In each of the cellars of these six cottages (and the condition was said to be common to the unoccupied as well as the occupied cottages) there were from 6 inches to 8 inches depth of water. This, I was told by the inhabitants, was the ordinary state of the cellars. With perverse ingenuity (as will presently be seen) the proprietor has placed a pump at the extremity of the cottages nearest the street, by means of which the water can be pumped out of the cellars. But as to dry the cellars in this manner entails no small amount of labour upon the occupants of the cottages, the pump is rarely had recourse to. The yard is not drained opposite these cottages except by the surface, and even the arrangements for surface drainage are most defective. Slops and other liquid refuse lodge in an imperfect channel opposite the cottages, and here and there spread out into filthier puddles, not the less offensive and indicative of neglect that they have been partially hidden by boulders.

Between the six cottages described and the street intervene, in the succession given, sundry pigsties; a large middenstead at the level of the yard, with attached privy; a foul smelling inclosure and outhouse joined to the slaughter-house of a pork-butcher; then a lair and cart-shed combined; next another midden, with a series of four privies, three locked, one open and inexpressibly foul; a slaughter-house follows, with a stable adjoining; and, finally, two cottages. A water stand-pipe is fixed near the slaughter-house last mentioned, and a pump stands opposite the two cottages at the entrance of the yard. The state of the surface is somewhat better at the lower part of the yard than at the upper; but here also it is so defective that the liquid refuse from the lower slaughter-house (as I witnessed myself) forms offensive pools as it flows across the yard towards the opening of a drain, which runs from opposite the slaughter-house to the common sewer in Kirkgate. The prolongation of this drain to the upper part of the yard, or of a drain laid at a proper depth, would prevent the flooding of the six upper cottages with water.

The whole state of this yard argues the most serious neglect of duty on the part of the Local Board of Health. Its proper drainage ought long ago to have been seen to. The crowding together of slaughter-houses, privies, middensteads, and cottages under conditions which renders it difficult to control any noxious influence which might arise from them, called and still calls for the utmost vigilance on the part of the local authority, and for the strictest exercise of the power entrusted to it to ameliorate such influence. But, except attention to the general cleanliness of the slaughter-houses, no proper measures have been taken to remedy a state of things which may be described as most reprehensible.

Sunderland Yard requires but brief comment. At the time of my visit it presented less for remark that other yards in the vicinity. As compared with these it was not easy to understand for what reason it was particularly mentioned in the complaints. The houses are much shut in, and the privies and middensteads placed beneath one of the railway arches were filthy and badly constructed, one of the privies opening towards the front of the houses.

Of other yards in Kirkgate, in a worse sanitary state than Sunderland Yard, I would mention the Spotted Leopard (formerly Spotted Dog) Yard and Day's Yard. The former is a narrow alley, badly channelled, with the privies and middenstead at the upper end. The channels and middensteads were alike foul, and from the latter exhaled an abominable excrementitious odour, filling the upper portion of the yard.

Day's Yard, on the east side of Kirkgate, is a long, narrow, closed court, of about 110 feet in length, and six and a half feet in width throughout the greatest part. The south side of the yard is at a lower level than the north, and is separated from the former by a low wall, the space between the wall and the doors of the houses measuring 3 feet. Each division of the yard is entered by a separate passage from Kirkgate. The southern division contains four cottages, or rather three, the first tenement forming a part of the house which fronts to Kirkgate, and beneath which the entrance passage runs. The second and third tenements were unoccupied at the time of the inspection; the fourth was in the occupation of a family consisting of three persons, who had lived there several years. Beyond this cottage is a small open, unpaved space, sodden with filth, littered with rubbish, and in which privies and a middenstead are placed, both the former and the latter in a foul state. The exit of the surface drain within this space was choked and a pool of liquid formed above, the stench was said to be well nigh unbearable at times. The north division of the yard contains seven cottages, all of which were occupied but one. The population of this side numbered thirty. The two cottages at the upper extremity of the yard face to the north, and are approached from the main yard by a narrow passage. At the end of these cottages, in a small space, shut off from the yard by double doors, are a single privy and a middenstead for the use of the whole seven cottages. In front of the two end cottages, and a little over three feet from their doors, the Local Board of Health has recently permitted to be built a brick wall about eight feet high. This wall acts as a screen, which cuts off to a great extent the scanty advantages in light and air which these cottages before possessed ov er the remainder in the yard. From the radical defects of arrangement of Day's Yard, neither the light nor the air can get into it without the one being dimmed and the other polluted.

Talbot Yard is a long, narrow yard running between North Street [sic] and Saville Street. The defects in this yard which call for remark, are (1) a collection of ashes and rubbish opposite the malt-kiln; (2) a dung-heap at the level of, and open to the roadway towards the Saville Street extremity of the yard; (3) the condition of the middenstead and privy in a small court, on the opposite side of the yard nearly facing this dung-heap; and (4) the condition and position of the privies and middensteads in the court which opens both into the Talbot Yard and into Old Crown Yard. One of the middensteads referred to is placed immediately beneath the scullery window of a cottage. The complaint regarding the state of this yard, referred particularly to a large dung-receptacle in the yard surrounded by a high wall. This was stated, when complained of, to be so loaded with horse and pig dirt, that the liquid manure flowed over the walls and formed large pools in the pathway.

In Providence Street there is a yard known as Wood's Yard. This yard is entirely shut in, except at the point where a passage opens, which traverses the houses facing to Providence Street. There are four cottages on each side of the yard, and formerly there was a fifth on the north side. One of the cottages on the latter side is a registered common lodging-house. The yard is about 70 feet in length, and 20 feet in breadth at the widest part. At the extremity, furtherest from the entrance, privies have been built, with shallow pits; but they have never been used. They were disapproved of by the Local Board of Health, and closed. In place of them, and with the approval of the Local Board, the fifth cottage on the north side has been converted into a privy in the following fashion: The entire front has been taken out, and the upper chamber floor removed. Upon the stone-flagged floor of the lower room a privy of four separate compartments has been erected, each compartment with a single aperture, corresponding with apertures in the floor below. The privy is arranged at right angles to the former front of the cottage, and behind the structure the flooring had been cut away, so as to give access to the cellar beneath, converted by this arrangement into the privy-pit and middenstead for the yard. Anything more revolting and wrong-headed than this arrangement it would be difficult to conceive. Properly to cleanse the cellar is impossible; and to have converted it to its present use, regardless of the foundations of the neighbouring cottages, cannot be justified.

The lodging-house in Wood's Yard has two windows in the rear. These look upon the back of a row of houses recently built by a Mr Robinson. The privies and combined privy-pits and middenstead of these houses are placed against the back of the lodging-house, adjoining cottage and privy-transformed-cottage in Wood's Yard. Now, the position of the privies is such, that a small window in the living-room of the lodging-house looks point blank upon the entrances to two; and a large window, permitting through ventilation of one of the sleeping-rooms of the lodging-house is placed above, and only a little to the right (looking from within) of the privy-pit and middenstead. To open the window is to admit the effluvium from the ordure and house-refuse; to keep the upper one closed is to destroy the only means of properly ventilating the sleeping-room. Closed or unclosed the stench from the privy-pits and midden penetrates into the house. The position of these privies and middenstead was approved by the Local Board of Health (Figures 18-19).

Figure 18. Briggs Yard, Northgate.
The John Goodchild Collection.

Figure 19. Barratt's Yard, Northgate.
The John Goodchild Collection.

The instances are numerous in which privies and middensteads are placed in immediate contact with the walls of houses. The danger of soakage into the dwellings, particularly when the walls are constructed of brick, is great An instance may be given from the locality under consideration. The backs of certain cottages in Barratt's Yard form the boundary of Wood's Yard furthest from the entrance. In one of the cottages referred to, about twelve months before the time of my inspection, a rapidly fatal case of acute fever-poisoning took place. This case was attended by Mr Lawson Tait, and he states that the attack unquestionably originated from the pollution of the atmosphere of the house, by the soaking of excremitious matter through the rear wall into the cellar. At the back of the house was a receptacle, now closed, for house and other refuse, and the liquid abominations from this receptacle had penetrated the walls of the cottage.

In the early twentieth century the conditions in yards were still causing concern. Thomas Gibson in his Notes on Public Health in Wakefield during the nineteenth century and from 1901 to 1935 refers to the Reports compiled by Dr Netten Radcliffe, in 1857 and 1869, and Gibson comments

It is worthy of note that many of the yards, whose houses are unfavourably commented on in a report written 66 years ago, have continued to exist until recent times, and indeed a few of them, though scheduled for clearance at an early date, still exist.

Of his own experience Gibson writes:

> *Yards were largely unpaved, privies and tub closets still abounded and the water supply had frequently to be obtained from a common stand pipe. ....In 1903 I represented 13 houses as unfit, and 12 of them were closed, but in the following year, when I represented 6, none were closed. Then in 1905, after I had made an extensive personal inspection of the older dwelling-houses, I had the temerity to represent 88 houses as the worst of a bad lot. The Sanitary Committee, after it had recovered from the shock, decided that 14 houses should be closed, but 9 of these 14 were eventually re-occupied after some repairs had been carried out.*
>
> *The passing of the Housing and Town Planning Act of 1909 did arouse a little more activity in housing matters, particularly in the direction of inspection and repair work. In 1913, I represented under this Act, the Westgate Insanitary Area, comprising Spawforth's and Tidswell's Yards, with some 20 houses, and in 1914 an Order was obtained to clear the area. Owing to the intervention of the War, the area was not actually cleared until 1925-6.*

In fact, perusal of the Council Minutes shows that in 1905 Gibson, the Medical Officer of Health had, in addition to his routine reports at each Sanitary Committee meeting, presented at virtually every meeting a list of houses which he considered unsatisfactory. In April of that year his annual report refers to two houses in Brickmaker yard: in one six people lived in the two-room dwelling, in the other nine people: parents and their children ranging from a baby to adults shared the two rooms, all nine sleeping in four beds in one of the rooms. After an inspection he reported on various yards off Stanley Road, Greenhill, Road and Jacob's Well Lane, of which

	Number of houses
Damp	56
Dilapidated	13
Dirty	25
Badly ventilated	59
Overcrowded	41
Without sinks	40
Without piped water	30
Tub closets	30
Privy Closets	10
Unpaved yards	7

In the weeks following the presentation of his annual report Gibson reported on unsatisfactory conditions, especially lack of water supply and drainage, affecting seven houses in Shaw Yard, eight in Rhodes, three in Beaumont's, three in Baxendale's, three in Briggs', fourteen in Library Yard, four in Clayton, five in the Three Tuns, four in Spurr, four in Firth, eight in White Swan, two in Fenton Heald's, thirteen in Volunteer and seven in Harrison's.

The condition of Spawforth and Tidswell's Yards had already been brought to the notice of that Committee by 1911 at the latest, but discussion was adjourned. The same matter seems to have been raised at virtually every meeting during 1912, procrastination seems to have been the order of the day and various devices were employed to this effect. Discussions were adjourned, sub-committees created, reports sought, and the matter was still being adjourned in October of 1912.

During this same year the Sanitary Committee refused to grant a licence for a slaughter-house in Howarth's Yard in Westgate, but granted such licences – for pigs only – in Small Page (sic), Baxendale's, Holt's and Albion Yard; at the same time licences for slaughter-houses, without restriction, were granted to unnamed yards in Thornes Lane and Doncaster Road.

Licences were also granted to keep 400 gallons of petroleum in two-gallon cans in Holts Yard, 100 gallons in a yard at 30 Ings Road, 200 in a yard off York St, and various amounts in other yards - Old Crown Yard, Foresters' Arms Yard at Sandal, York Hotel Yard and at 48 Ings Rd, whilst 112 lbs of carbide is licensed in the Stafford Arms Mews.

In his manuscript *History of Wakefield*, S Baines mentions that two cottages in Prospect Yard, owned by Joseph Wainwright have, built into their front walls, 'several fragments' consisting of 'mullions and other ornamental work' taken from the old Chantry Chapel during its ill-fated restoration of the 1840s.

The same author mentions the existence of a Fox's or Foxes Yard, which forms part of the footpath route to Thornes; later he defines this as being either an alternative name for or a part of Lord Rodney Yard.

In 1947 a decision was made to rename some yards, Albion Yard off Kirkgate became Noel Yard, Fawcett's Yard off Ingwell Street became Wallace Yard, and Wilson's Yard off Kirkgate became Jackson's Yard.

Only a handful of yards have survived to the end of the twentieth century. The vestigial remains of many yards are visible to those who walk round the city centre today; some of them still bear their original names, but most are totally anonymous and they bear no resemblance

Figure 20. Thompson's Yard, Westgate, in the early 1980s, with the principal door to the Gissings' home on the left.

to the yard of former times; often they are reduced to a passage way between two buildings, leading nowhere or simply providing a shortcut for impatient humanity; most just provide access to the rear of the buildings fronting the street, attempts have been made to commercialise or gentrify a couple of yards. The Woolpacks Yard is bright and clean with an entrance to the pub, Thompson's Yard, with the Gissing house preserved, retains at first glance some appearance of a traditional yard, but beyond the Gissing centre all is changed (Figure 20). The White Horse Yard retains some of the character of an old yard with its haphazard structure, but the barred windows and the fire escapes from upper storeys give the lie to that first impression – and the discarded coke cans and glue containers are strictly late twentieth century (Figure 21). A map produced in the 1990s by Wakefield Metropolitan District Council shows only fourteen yards surviving (and one of those has been omitted from the index), and an OS map published in 1996 shows seventeen - there is some overlap between these two lists. Those still, apparently extant, at the time of writing in 1999, include:

Avison (Kirkgate)
Brewers Arms (Westgate)
Cass (Kirkgate)
Dixon's (Kirkgate)
George & Crown (Silver Street)
Gill's (Northgate)
Governors (Stanley Road)
Holt's (Westgate)
Navigation (Kirkgate)
Prospect (behind the Theatre Royal and Opera House)
Rodney (forms one of the entrances to The Ridings)
Saw (Westgate)

Smallpage (between Union St and Brook St)
Swan (Westgate, formerly *The Swan with Two Necks*)
Talbot and Falcon (from Northgate to the Bus Station)
Thompson's (Westgate)
White Horse (Westgate)
Wild's (off Thornhill St)
Woolpacks (Westgate)

Also listed are a total of thirty-four yards in the whole of the rest of the Wakefield Metropolitan District one in Stanley, three in Castleford, ten in Ossett, eleven in Horbury, six in Pontefract, and three in the Sitlington area.

In the mid-nineteenth century the yards seem to have had quite different characters, some, notably the Manor House Yard house not only officials connected with that eponymous institution, but other attorneys, land surveyors and agents, The Woolpacks Yard contained, exclusively wool-related trades, as did the nearby Star Yard. In 1837 the Great Bull Yard housed a blacksmith, a cabinet maker and a woolstapler, the Old Crown – a blacksmith and a coachmaker, the Old Red Lion and the Old Wharf Yards each contained a maltster, Robinsons housed a printer, the Saw a blacksmith and a wheelwright. At the same time Rodney Yard contained dwellings and an insurance agent, whilst the Windmill was home to the widest

Figure 21. White Horse Yard looking towards Westgate, 2001.

range of trades - an attorney, a currier, a plumber and glazier and an iron and brass founder. Other yards contain mostly artisans, smiths, painters, wheelwrights, braziers, coopers or carpenters. Another yard contained, for a short while at least, two cow-keepers! In 1822 there is a fruiterer at the top of Church Yard and a grocer on the corner of the same yard; apart from these and those afore-mentioned cow-keepers there seem to be virtually no food-related services or shops in yards, nor are there many whose trade would, presumably, be mainly with the female gentry or at least better-off ladies of the town, such as milliners or dressmakers. Perhaps surprisingly The White Swan in 1822, and Crowthers, and the Woolpacks in 1830 house schools - additionally several school masters have dwellings in yards at this time and in subsequent directories. In at least two directories – 1837 and 1842 – the Great Bull Yard houses an Independent minister of religion and a horse dealer, though in 1834 that yard had contained a wood turner and an organ builder. In 1834 Crowther's Yard off Northgate housed an artist.

In the *1892 Directory* at about 72 Kirkgate there is located a Pitt's Yard; by 1904 this has disappeared and in the same vicinity Jackson's Arcade has appeared. This seems to have had two or three small shops on each side at the street end, with the sides from 7-21 and 6-22 (and presumably across the end of the Arcade) occupied by Jackson's stores, house furnishers. This metamorphosis of a yard into an arcade presumably represents a major change in image. I have never seen a postcard published depicting any Wakefield yards, but a postcard of Jackson's Arcade survives – and has been published in the 1999 Wakefield Hospice Calendar – it looks like a very smart shopping area and seems to suggest a pride in the place which is unlikely to have been generated by a yard – I have been told that there was such an excellent music-shop there that it was a favourite shopping area in the nineteen-twenties and 'thirties.

Footnote:

The writer would be delighted to receive any additional information on yards (or even corrections to the information provided).

Bibliography

1. Gibson, T *Notes on public health in Wakefield during the 19th century and from 1901-1935*, Wakefield, 1937.
2. Ranger, W *Report to the General Board of Health on a preliminary enquiry, 1852.*
3. Radcliffe, J N *Sanitary administration and state of Wakefield, 1869.*
4. Baines, S *History of Wakefield*, MSS, 1915.

2. OSSETT GOLF CLUB 1909-1925

by Brian Wallis

FOR MORE THAN NINETY YEARS golf has been played in Ossett.

The Low Laithes Golf Club was formed in 1925 but for some considerable time before that a golf club existed in the town. It was thanks to the efforts of the members of this club that Low Laithes came into being.

The exact date of the formation of the Ossett Golf Club is not known. According to the secretary's report presented to the first annual meeting, the club was formed in November 1909, fifteen years before the game was first played at Low Laithes where the Ossett members moved in 1925. The report finds confirmation by the Ossett Observer newspaper of 13 November, 1909 which announced:

> *A proposal is afoot and it is taking practical shape for the founding of a golf club in Ossett. A committee is engaged in preparing a scheme and it is thought to be possible that the club will be formed.*
>
> *The suggestion is to prepare a course across the fields in the neighbourhood of Springmill. Negotiations are taking place and we hear that thirty acres of land are available and that an expert who has been consulted considers that a good nine-hole course can be arranged. There appears to be no lack of prospective members.*

The land on which the Ossett Club laid out its course was situated

Figure 1. Looking across to a part of Ossett golf course from the present Springmill course, Queen's Drive, Ossett.

Figure 2. A part of the site of the former Ossett golf course, Broadowler Lane.

between Springmill and the Wakefield, Batley and Bradford branch line of the Great Northern Railway. Flushdyke railway station was to the north (Figures 1 and 2). To the south was Greatfield Road and Broadowler Lane. An ordnance survey map of 1922 shows the position of the golf course on land subsequently used for the development of Towngate (Figure 3).

As was the case with the Horbury and District Golf Club formed at Coxley Valley, Middlestown, two years earlier and practically all golf clubs at this time, the principal founders of the Ossett club were local professional and business men. Among them was Arthur Jessop of Green Lea, Healey Road, Ossett, a mungo and marino manufacturer of Springfield Mills. He was the club's first president.

Figure 3. Ordnance Survey map of 1922 showing the Ossett golf course and the original club house on Broadowler Lane.

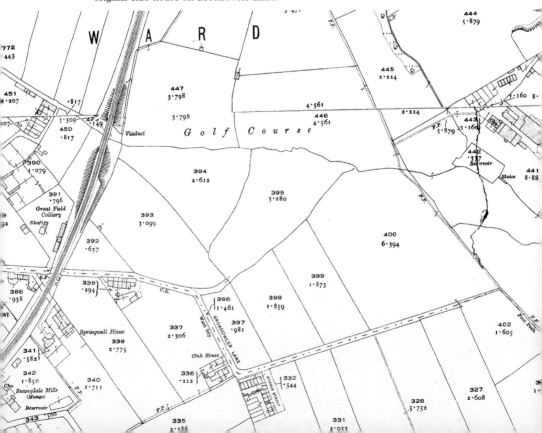

In 1910 he donated the Jessop Cup, afterwards presented to the Low Laithes club and which is still competed for by its members (Figure 4). Henry Glover Myers of Greatfield was the Ossett club's treasurer from 1910 to 1924 and president in 1924, the last full year of its existence. Oliver Myers, a rag and mungo merchant, Fieldhead and Church Street, was the first secretary, from 1911 to 1916. In 1911 he was elected the first captain, having proved his merits as a golfer by winning the inaugural play-off for the Jessop Cup, a feat he repeated in the following year. Among other

Figure 4. The Jessop Cup.

members were Albert Fearnside Glover, Bank Street, John Henry Glover JP, Northfield House, who was captain in 1913-14 and president in 1920-21, Albert Myers, the Chestnuts, Station Road, Councillors George Frederick Wilson JP and George H Briggs, a woollen cloth manufacturer, Storrs Hill Road, Arthur Rhodes, secretary 1917-19, and Doctors W L R Wood, George Symers Mill, Wesley Street, and Alexander Diggles La Touche, Prospect House, Station Road, Albert Egerton Mottram, Rose Lea, Headlands Road, manager of the Ossett Gas Works, Healey Road, Thomas Glover Brook, president 1917-19, and Bernard Brook, both of Kent Villa, Station Road, Albert Mitchell Lawrence, Dale Street, solicitor, John Pearson, Market Place, manager of the London City and Midland Bank, William Muir Oddie, accountant, the club auditor, J H Winterbottom, captain 1915-1920, and Harry Sykes of Earlsheaton, all of whom were in attendance at the first annual meeting in 1911.

A H Rhodes, Alfred Brook and A E Mottram were founder

Figure 5. The house on the left was the first to be used as a clubhouse, 1909-1912.

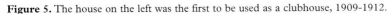

members of the Horbury and District Golf Club in 1907 and it was possibly through them and other members there that the idea to form a golf club in Ossett was first suggested.

The first annual meeting of the Ossett Golf Club was held at the Temperance Hall on Tuesday 17 January, 1911. Arthur Jessop, the president, was in the chair and there was an attendance of about thirty members. The secretary reported that after the club had been formed in November 1909 it had been met at once with a great deal of success, a large number of new members being elected at each meeting of the committee up to April 1910 when the membership had reached 126. It being the first year, a great amount of work was necessary on the course and in the clubhouse (Figure 5). Competitions had caused a great deal of interest among members. The first competition was on 2 July, 1910, a medal, which was won by Harry Glover Myers. Oliver Myers was the first winner of the Jessop Cup, defeating J W Winterbottom in the final round of a matchplay competition.

The accounts for the first fourteen months of the club's existence showed the total income to be £230 13s 4d, including £212 from members' subscriptions (gentlemen £2 2s and ladies £1 1s). Expenditure amounted to £239 15s 6d, including £78 outlay on the construction of the course, this item covering the cost of purchasing rollers and lawn mowers, erecting bridges and stiles. Rents, rates, caretaker's wages and other expenditure in the club-house, including the fitting of lockers, came to £161 15s 10d. The excess of income over expenditure was £9 2s 6d. Arthur Jessop was re-elected president. Dr La Touche, Dr Mill, Alfred Mitchell Lawrence, Thomas G Brook and Alfred Brook were elected vice-presidents. It was these gentlemen who subsequently donated the Vice-Presidents' Trophy, competed for later in 1911 and won by L Varley. Hubert Taylor was the winner of the first monthly medal winners' final.

A further nineteen members were elected to the club in 1911, two

Figure 6. The house in Broadowler Lane used as the second clubhouse, 1912-1925.

new holes were opened for play, and during the next two years a total of £280 was spent on the course making new tees and greens, and a horse-drawn mowing machine was obtained which 'greatly improved the fairways'.

In 1912 a professional, Allen Bellwood, was engaged, interclub matches were arranged for the first time, with teams from Cross Gates and South Leeds clubs, and in October the ladies played their first competition, Mrs J Winterbottom being the winner of a medal competition. Mrs A Myers and Miss Mitchell were the other two returns.

Despite a further £48 spent on furnishing a new clubhouse, which the members moved into in 1912, there was a balance in hand at the end of the year of £9 6s 7d and at the annual meeting in 1913 another successful year was reported. By this time the club had joined the Yorkshire Union of Golf Clubs (Figure 6). Arthur Jessop having for business reasons declined to be reappointed president, his place was taken by Thomas Brook. J H Glover was elected captain.

Allen Bellwood was the Ossett club's only professional. Prior to his appointment he had been with the Dewsbury District Golf Club. His older brother, Frank Bellwood, resigned as professional there in 1909 on taking a post in America.

During the First World War, when the Ossett club's course was closed, Allen Bellwood returned to Dewsbury, remaining there as professional until 1919 when he rejoined the Ossett club. In 1924 he left Ossett to rejoin his brother as assistant at the Garden City Golf Club on Long Island, New York. In appreciation of his services he was presented with a gold wrist watch 'suitably inscribed' by the president, Harry G Myers. What happened to the Bellwoods after 1924 is not known.

The club continued to progress and the two years prior to the First World War were its most successful up to this time. In 1913 the number of gentlemen members increased. There was a record number of entries in the club competitions and for the first time it became necessary to arrange a second-division monthly medal. Income from visitors' green fees in 1914 was also more than in any previous year. During the year the lease on the course was renewed for another five years whilst two of the members of the committee, Harry Sykes of Earlsheaton and Bernard Brook of Ossett, died. The secretary, Oliver Myers, was the club's leading player in this period. By the time of his appearance in the monthly medal winners' final in 1914, he had reduced his handicap of fourteen in 1910 to scratch. Playing in the first division of the monthly medal competition in July

1914, he returned a gross score of seventy-three, a record for the course, three strokes under bogey. J Holmes (handicap 6), S Pollitt (8), H White (8), J H Glover (8) and A H Rhodes (9) were the other leading players. All played in the inter-club matches. Arthur Rhodes had a handicap of 8 at the Horbury and District Golf Club. He was elected an honorary life member there in 1942 and was captain of the club in 1928 and president from 1933 to 1935.

Following the outbreak of war on 1 August 1914, the Ossett club, after five years of steady growth, went into decline. At the annual meeting in 1915 it was reported that several members had joined HM Forces. While there was an increase in the number of ladies and juniors, the number of gentlemen members had fallen from eighty-five in 1913 to seventy-one. The membership continued to fall (to 111 at the end of 1915) and expenditure for the year ending 31 December was £66 in excess of income. A similar loss was reported in the following year when it was decided that the amount of the deficit should be voluntarily subscribed by the members. Later in the year Williams, the steward, volunteered for the army.

While competitions continued throughout 1915, and during the year matches were played in aid of the Red Cross and the Prince of Wales National Relief Fund, for patriotic reasons the course was closed between the months of April and August from 1916 to 1918 for the growing of crops. As a result of this and war conditions generally, many members left to join other clubs which remained open. In 1917 the club was granted the use of the course at Dewsbury at reduced rates for those of its members that remained. Oliver Myers, after eight years as secretary, was replaced by A H Rhodes.

After the war Ossett's fortunes were changed with the introduction of what was called a 'revival scheme' and the formation of the club into a limited company. Work in putting the course back in order was commenced early in 1919 and Bellwood, who resigned from the Dewsbury club, was re-engaged as 'professional and groundsman'. In October a notice was placed in the social columns of the *Ossett Observer* inviting subscriptions for

> *£1 ordinary shares in the Ossett Golf Club Limited, nominal capital £1,000, no allotment to be made unless a minimum £400 is secured.*

With the annual subscriptions remaining at the old rates it was hoped that the club would soon return to a strong position with regard to its membership. Competition for the club's main trophies, the Jessop Cup and the Vice-President's Trophy, was to recommence and the social side of the club's activities was to be emphasised (Figure 7).

Figure 7. The Kaye Cup (left), the Jessop Cup and the Vice-President's Trophy (rose bowl).

The scheme was a success and at a meeting on 22 October it was reported that sufficient shares in the company had been taken to justify proceeding with the allotment. On 1 January 1920 the Ossett Golf Club Limited was registered.

But the first year after the club's revival was not a good one and it was very soon realised that subscriptions at levels set in 1909 were nowhere near high enough to cover expenditure, a loss of £56 15s 4d being reported to the annual meeting on 31 January 1921, the first to be held in four years. The total income amounted to £457 5s 11d. Against this, expenditure was £514 1s 3d and included rent and rates of £160 12s 3d (against £85 2s 9d in 1913), upkeep of course £112 17s 9d (£38 8s 2d), professional's and caretaker's wages £208 16s (£58 3s professional's wages only in 1913). Membership at this time was 166. After much discussion and in view of the poor financial position, it was decided to increase the subscriptions of playing members to £3 3s for gentlemen and £1 10s 6d for ladies and juniors. The election of officers followed and, after an amendment to the rules, the question of allowing golf to be played on Sundays was discussed, although this was afterwards found not to be possible.

Despite the ban on Sunday golf and fears that the increase in subscriptions might lead to a loss of members, the number of gentlemen, ladies and juniors belonging to the club at the end of 1921 was 174 and the financial statement for the year showed it to be flourishing. In September the club had asked for, and been granted, permission by the Ossett Corporation to use the town's coat of arms as its club badge.

Figure 8. Ossett Town Hall in 2001.

The club continued to flourish and to gain in membership, 189 at the end of 1922, its highest recorded level. During the year extensive alterations to the course were carried out and in 1923 sufficient funds were available for the purchase of additional furniture for the clubhouse including a few deck chairs which added greatly to the comfort of members. In club competitions, E Scorah won the Vice-Presidents' Trophy, now called the Rose Bowl, while Mrs G Briggs was successful in the ladies' gold medal. Bogey for the course was reduced from seventy-six to seventy-two . On the social side, a whist drive and dance held in Ossett Town Hall was very successfully carried out. (Figure 8).

Between 1920 and 1924 these events at the Town Hall were a feature of life at the old Ossett Golf Club.

In 1924, golf in Ossett reached another turning point in its short career with the decision to form a new golf club in the town. The idea for a new 18-hole golf club was first discussed by the Ossett members early in 1924. They had already seen the land which was for sale and had obtained a report from Dr McKenzie, a golf-course architect, as to its suitability. They had, however, not been able to raise the necessary money (£2,000). But after a match at Heath Common, the idea was brought to the attention of Councillor James Walter Watson of Wakefield, a member of Heath Golf Club, who agreed to purchase the land and lease it to the new club (Figure 9).

By the end of July 1924 plans had been drawn up for the construction of the new course in the neighbourhood of the Ossett

Figure 9. The former clubhouse at Heath, in 2001.

club at Low Laithes Farm, Flushdyke. The name of the club was to be the Ossett and District Golf Club, although this was afterwards changed because of its similarity to the name of the old club. On 14 August at a public meeting in the Town Hall with Julian Thornton, a former captain of the club, presiding, it was stated that James Watson, in addition to leasing the land, had very generously offered to pay for the exterior alterations to the clubhouse, a former farm house. So the new club had to find only the cost of laying out the course and the furnishings and interior alterations to the clubhouse (Figure 10).

Sunday golf, not previously allowed, would be permitted.

A good many members of the old club had promised their support and it was expected that a number would be recruited from other clubs in the district, Heath, Horbury and District, and Hanging Heaton whose courses were of nine holes.

By the time of a second public meeting, again held in the Town Hall, on 30 August, more than half the capital necessary for the construction of the new course had been acquired. On 24 December the land was secured and on 1 January, 1925 the Low Laithes Golf Club came into being. On Friday 23 January the old Ossett Golf Club Limited was

Figure 10. The premises at Low Laithes before alterations. *Ken Bartlett.*

wound up at a meeting of creditors at Springstone House.

The first meeting of the Low Laithes club was held on 5 April, 1925 and on 30 May the official opening of the clubhouse took place. In all five trophies were donated to the Low Laithes club in its first year including the Jessop Cup and the Vice-Presidents' Trophy (Rose Bowl) donated by the old club, and the Kaye Cup, a new award presented by Sam Kaye, a member of the Ossett club and one of the first vice-presidents of Low Laithes.

Of the other Ossett members to take an active part in the formation of the Low Laithes Golf Club, James Webster was the first treasurer while Albert Fearnside, H Fogg, H Holmes, Anlaby Pickles, Harold Moss and Julian Thornton were all elected to the first committee. H Holmes (1922) and H Fogg (1924) were both former captains of the old club. Julian Thornton, captain in 1923, was elected to that office at Low Laithes three times, in 1925, 1926 and 1933, and was twice its president, in 1934 and 1935. B P Wilson was another of the first vice-presidents at Low Laithes. Mrs Knowles, Mrs Pickard, Mrs Holmes, Mrs Wilson, Mrs Pickles, Mrs Fogg and Mrs Kaye, all members of the old club, were elected to the first ladies' committee at Low Laithes.

It was with thanks to James Walker Watson and the efforts of these members of the Ossett club that Low Laithes came into being. Two other members of the old club were J Marsden and Percy Fogg who were elected captains and presidents at Low Laithes in the 1930s and 1940s.

While the Heath (1911-1940) and Horbury and District (1907-1965) golf clubs have disappeared, Low Laithes has celebrated its 75th anniversary in 2000. In 2009 golf in Ossett will celebrate its centenary.

A full list of members and lists of trophies and winners are to be included in an extended account by the author to be published at some future date. Also to follow is a history of golf on Heath Common.

Sources

Issues of *The Wakefield Express* and *The Ossett Observer*.
Handbooks of the Yorkshire Union of Golf Clubs.
Ordnance survey map 1922.
Harry Marshall, *Sixty Years and More: A History of Low Laithes 1925-1985.*
Kelly's *Directories* 1908, 1922.
Land registry records of the Ossett Borough Council 1909-1925, West Yorkshire Archive Service.
B Wallis, *Echoes from an Old Fairway: A History of the Horbury and District Golf Club 1907-1965,* (1986)

3. THE BADSWORTH HUNT: ITS ORIGINS AND DEVELOPMENT UP TO C.1918

by John Goodchild

FOXHUNTING AND RACING are perhaps the oldest nationally spread sports in England. Cricket and archery are, indeed, old sports, but on an organised basis and covering most of the country fox-hunting comes first, along with horse-racing: organised football, golf and tennis are in England essentially Victorian sports. The thrill of the chase, the unpredictability of the fox, the riding of the horse across ditches and hedges, not to mention the socialising appeal of the hunt itself, its organisation and its excitement, its before-and-after social mixing, have appealed since the seventeenth century, as they do today.

The Badsworth Hunt is one of Yorkshire's oldest hunts and it remains today a conspicuous feature of the county's sporting scene. Its territory extends from the valley of the Calder in the west to the Ouse in the east, with very different soils covered in that wide tract; it covered land owned by major landowners to that owned by small freeholders, and it has always attracted men and women from a wide variety of occupations and social standings, from farmers and country gentry to – as followers on foot etc – townies and colliers. The area hunted by the Badsworth is covered – and that most artistically and beautifully – by the map of the Badsworth Hunt country which was published in 1826.

The origins of the Badsworth Hunt are difficult to determine in regard to the exact date and place and personnel, but they would seem to originate in a number of onetime independent gentlemen's packs of hounds which were ultimately amalgamated and made of wider use. By the end of the seventeenth century, the Wentworth family of Woolley Hall had their own hounds which were, at least in part, maintained by tenants on their estates as one of the so-called boons, which were obligations on their tenants in addition to money rent payments (Figure 1). A lease of 1697 provides for the keeping and feeding of 'one dog hound or beagle as he or they (the landlord) shall please to send so to be kept,' a clause which perhaps significantly is not included in a prior lease in 1684, while a further

Figure 1. A Victorian print of Woolley Hall. *The John Goodchild Collection.*

lease of 1710 provides for the keeping and well feeding – for the three farms now in lease, at Notton – of 'Three hounds or beagles' for Wentworth's use. It may well be that hunting with packs of dogs was coming into use among local gentlemen at the end of the seventeenth century: similar provisions are made in the eighteenth century leases of farms on the Newland estate near Wakefield, the estate whose later holder, Sir Edward Smith, baronet, was to have kennels built there and to be himself for some years in the 1790s Master of the Badsworth Hunt (Figure 2). Certainly by 1708 William Wentworth of Woolley (1675-1729), who succeeded his father in 1686, had his own pack of hounds, while his nephew and successor Godfrey Wentworth (who died in 1789 aged eighty-four), who was for some time one of the two Members of Parliament for York, maintained a private pack of hounds too.

The Wentworths of Woolley Hall were not unique in their possession of this sporting facility, and it is said to have been the pack of Thomas Bright of Badsworth Hall, sometime MP for Pontefract, which formed the original nucleus of the hunt which derived its name from his home, Badsworth Hall (Figure 3). Bright had come of

Figure 2. Newland Hall. *The John Goodchild Collection.*

Figure 3. Badsworth Hall pictured in 1926. *The John Goodchild Collection.*

age in 1716, married an heiress in 1734, succeeded to the estates in 1735 and died in 1739, leaving an only daughter who married the great second Marquess of Rockingham, owner of the Wentworth Woodhouse estates and sometime Prime Minister. Bright's own father, however, John Liddell Bright (1671-1735), who owned the Badworth Hall estate to his death, was described as a 'famous breeder of beagles, spaniels and foxhounds... in this line of business he was an acknowledged Master and his dogs were in great demand.' The Hunt is claimed to have originated in 1720 or 1730. There is an old hunting ballad, 'An account of an excellent fox chase performed by Mr Bright's hounds,' dated 1730. In 1735 or 1739 the hunting country, lying within the Wapentakes of Osgoldcross and Agbrigg, centred respectively on Pontefract and Wakefield, was taken over by William Spencer (died 1756, aged sixty-seven) and then by John Spencer – Squire Spencer as he was known to all – of Cannon Hall near Barnsley who died unmarried in 1775 aged fifty-seven. He was described in 1835 by a descendant in title as 'respected, feared and trusted by all who knew him... like his father before him, he kept a first rate pack of fox-hounds, the ancestors of those afterwards celebrated as Lord Darlington's hounds.' He hunted with Francis Offley Edmunds of Worsbrough Hall, JP (1736-1825) and Sir John Kaye of Denby Grange near Wakefield; the latter was one of the post-hunting

Figure 4. Cannon Hall. *Kate Taylor.*

party at Cannon Hall, where twenty men at dinner drank sixty bottles of port, an average of three apiece (Figure 4). The huntsmen are said to have been off at five in the morning, and on John Spencer's last day as Master of the hunt, he found a fox at Haw Park near Wakefield and killed him at Bolsterstone on the Derbyshire border, a major day's horseback riding. A man of the name of Best was his huntsman, who, mounted on a very powerful but not very fast horse, would take great fences and then turn with a wink to remark to those who hesitated in following him, 'One moust mak' a bit of a lep now and agean'!

A Mr Spencer is said to have hunted the Badsworth country from 1739 until 1769: this must apply to both the father and the bachelor son who inherited in 1756. For a time the joint Mastership of the Badsworth Hunt was shared between John Spencer and his friend and relative John Stanhope, who lived from c1701 to 1769, the leading barrister on the Northern Circuit, also a bachelor, of Horsforth Hall near Leeds; the heir of both was their joint nephew, Walter Spencer Stanhope.

But there were other packs apart from those of the Spencers and 't'old lawyer', as he was known, John Stanhope. Sir Rowland Winn, the fourth baronet, of Nostell Priory near Wakefield (1706-1765; he succeeded his father in 1721) kept a pack of foxhounds about 1763; he was fond of hunting, reports a female relative, but kept his hounds as 'a sort of rallying point, that should draw around it the neighbouring gentlemen.' At much the same period, in fact in the 1750s, the Badsworth Hunt is claimed in another source to have originated at Cusworth Hall, near Doncaster, the seat of William Wrightson (born 1676, succeeded his brother 1724 and died 1760) (Figure 5). Apparently all these packs, by design or chance, coalesced into the Badsworth Hunt.

Just a little about the hounds of this period – and, indeed, about yet another local pack too – is revealed in the account book of the

Figure 5. Cusworth Hall. *Brian Elliott.*

Reverend James Torre, squarson of Snydale Hall near Wakefield since 1749. From 1754 he paid subscriptions, rising from two guineas a year to the four guineas he paid in 1760, to Sir George Dalston of Heath (Old) Hall, near Wakefield, whom he describes as 'Master of the Wakefield Hunt'. Torre bought a pointer bitch for two guineas, and in 1756 he paid the ferryman at Stanley Ferry, near Wakefield, two shillings for ferrying hounds for the hunt. He mentions two of his dogs, called Ponto and Basto; Ponto required training and he paid £1 1s 6d to 'Clint Dog Teacher at Aberford in full for teaching Ponto'.

The Hunt occasionally witnessed disasters as well as pleasures. Early in 1810, when the Earl of Darlington was Master of the Badsworth foxhounds, he sent a bagged fox to be turned out for the pleasure of the Wakefield Harriers, whose meet was at Park Lodge, just outside the town. The fox took down to the side of the Calder and then crossed the river above Kirkthorpe Dam. William Burrell, a cloth merchant living in South Parade in Wakefield, went into the river on horseback; his horse threw him and, despite all efforts – the river bank was unstable for helpers – he drowned and was interred in the catacombs of Westgate Chapel where his body remains.

Supporters of the Harriers and also of the Hunt in Wakefield at this time, as recorded by Henry Clarkson in

Figure 6. The vignette by Schwanfelder which decorates a corner of the map of the Badsworth Hunt Country. *The John Goochild Collection.*

Figure 7. Stapleton Hall, sketched by G Percy Rhodes for 'Memorials of a Yorkshire Parish'. *J S Fletcher (1914).*

his *Memories*, were the Whites, Rickabys, Todd Naylor, Lonsdale (brother of the later bishop of Lichfield). Scotts, Rayners, and others unnamed.

Henry Clarkson, who records the Burrell tragedy, was also co-surveyor of the private venture which published the splendid map of the Badsworth Hunt country in 1826, ornamented by a spirited vignette by the artist Schwanfelder, animal painter to George IV (Figure 6). The publication was a complete financial failure, claims Clarkson, despite taking Clarkson two years, 1823 to 1825, on his one half of the surveying work for it. The Master of the Hunt at that time was the Honourable Edward Robert Petre, living at Stapleton Park (Figure 7).

Another glimpse of the Hunt occurs in the biography of William Whiteley who was to grow up to become nationally, and even internationally, known as the Universal Provider from his huge London what we might now call supermarket in Westbourne Grove. Born at Agbrigg Farm near Wakefield, his family moved to Purston Jaglin, and young Whiteley is said to have hunted with the Badsworth at ten; he later recollected the little snow-white pony he rode, afraid of no five-barred gates, stone walls, high hedges or wide streams. In the Hunt he met, in the 1840s, Lord Hawke and his brother Stanhope Hawke, Charles Greaves (who weighed twenty stones) and the great John Gully, erstwhile prize fighter, horse racer, ex-MP, and colliery proprietor, who lived at Ackworth Park. Whiteley recalls of these days:

The members of the Hunt were very proud of me, and very kind, because they thought me a real good sportsman, as whenever the meet was anywhere near my home I was always there, no matter what the weather might be. And when, after a long run, we called at the nearest gentleman's house and had the usual crust of bread, piece of cheese, and horn of home-brewed ale, they always took care that I was not overlooked and had my full share, Mr Gully in particular paying me special attention.

Gully, indeed, gave the young huntsman a pony.

A rather more curious sight must have been the gypsies who, also in the 1840s, came annually to the Wentbridge area, especially in the hunting season. It was said that fifteen or twenty of them followed the Badsworth hounds, mounted on well-bred and spirited horses, the men sporting knee breeches, blue stockings, low shoes with silver buckles and short brown velvet jackets ornamented with brass buttons.

It would be tedious to outline the biographies of all those who were the Masters of the Badsworth Hunt, yet a few of them deserve some short notes on account of their activities or, indeed, their eccentricities, and a preliminary list of the masters may not come amiss. The list has been compiled from a variety of sources and by its very nature is almost certainly incomplete so far as the dates of the Mastership are concerned, for after all the hunt is a sporting rather than an adminstrative body, and until the end of the eighteenth century it was financed very largely by the Master rather than by hunt members: indeed the hunt as such belonged to the Master, and those who wished came along to it and were welcomed, decent behaviour alone being regarded as the necessary qualification:

Masters of the Badsworth Hunt: a preliminary list, 1769-1910, subject to amendment

1769-1783	Earl of Darlington
1783-1792	William Wrightson of Cusworth Park, Doncaster
1792-1795?	Sir Edward Smith of Newland Park, Wakefield
1795?-1798?	Sir Edward Smith and Godfrey Wentworth of Woolley Park, ?jointly
1798?-1802	Sir Thomas Pilkington of Chevet Park, Wakefield, ? jointly with Sir Rowland Winn of Nostell Priory, Wakefield
1802	Earl of Dartmouth
1803?-?1809?	3rd Earl of Darlington, later 1st Duke of Cleveland; lived locally when hunting, at Ackworth Moor Top.
1809?-1814	Sir William Gerard
1814?-1815	John Musters
1815-1817	Sir Bellingham Graham: left only 12 couples of hounds and 3 horses in the kennels

1817-1821	Thomas Bent Hodgson
1821-1826	Hon Edward Petre of Stapleton Park
1826?-1869?	4th Baron Hawke of Womersley Park
1869-1876	John Hope Barton of Stapleton Park
1876-1892	Charles Booth Elmsall Wright of Bolton Hall and Bilham House
1892-1895	Lt Col W J F Ramsden of Rogerthorpe Manor
1895-1902	John Skipworth Herbert Fullerton of Thrybergh Park
1902-1905	Charles Brook
1905-1908	Henry John Hope Barton of Stapleton Park
1908-1910	James Fountayne Montagu of High Melton Hall.

It is difficult to dwell upon the characters of these men, although much is known of some of them. Lord Hawke of Womersley Hall was the longest-serving Master by far, with his forty years and perhaps more in that office; he was described as being 'no great hound man nor yet the stuff of which great Masters are made' and he reduced hunting to two days a week and sold off ten couples of hounds, although when he died in 1869 it was as a result of a hunting accident. He kept excellent huntsmen, including Will Butler. Lord Hawke was fond of sounding the hunting horn incessantly, and on one occasion this huntsman exploded, declaring, 'Damn that horn, m'lord, I'll tell you when to blow it!'

Thomas Bent Hodgson was rather more typical of the nouveaux riches who were entering the Hunt – and incidentally probably making it more respectable, in the middle-class sense of less rowdy and less inebriated. As Master, 1817-1821, he was both young and impecunious, but he built up the hounds from the mere twelve couples left by his predecessor and was a splendid sportsman in the hunting line, before leaving the Badsworth for the Holderness Hunt 1824-1842, where he was a great success. His personal story is an interesting one, but perhaps not relevant in its detail to this study. He was elected West Riding Registrar of Deeds at Wakefield in 1842 , one of the West Riding's three great sinecures, which he held until his death in 1863.

The Badsworth Hunt seems to have had no kennels of its own until the nineteenth century, the hounds being apparently housed in the kennels of the Master. When Sir Edward Smith of Newland near Wakefield was Master, from 1792 to (probably) 1798 or later, he had his own kennels; a military man in his younger days who succeeded his father in 1789 at twenty, Sir Edward's steward wrote to him in

1790 informing him that the new kennels at Newland were coming on well in their building. In 1791 he had permission to hunt over the adjoining Smyth of Heath Hall estate, and in 1798 he paid tax on fifteen horses and a pack of hounds: he still had fourteen dogs in 1822. In the 1820s Sir Edward was a partner to an agreement whereby Lord Hawke, of Stapleton Park, would have £1,400 a year by subscription from the Hunt, plus the use of 'earth stopping covers and kennels'; Lord Hawke was master of the Badsworth Hunt from 1820 for forty years.

The financial basis on which the Hunt operated from at least the early nineteenth century was by subscription among formal members. If the earlier masters of the Hunt had earlier taken full fiscal responsibility, from 1809 (when Sir William Gerard, the eleventh baronet, a young man of then about twenty-six from Lancashire, temporarily forsook his longtime family staghound pack to hunt the Badsworth country) large sums were raised by subscription. A then huge £2,100 and more was spent, used for stopping earths, repairing old covers and making new ones, building hunting access bridges over streams, and other unspecified costs, all for 'purposes promotive of fox-hunting' for the Badsworth Hunt. As well as participating landowners' subscriptions, there were more minor ones from persons lower in the social scale and of between five and fifteen guineas which were paid by twenty named persons, all male: a couple of parsons, a doctor, two colonels, a number of minor country estate owners or tenants, a major Wakefield cloth merchant (John Naylor), and a Mr Carr, perhaps the Wakefield lawyer of that name.

In 1813 Sir William Gerard was being pressed to bring the hounds into the Badsworth area each year on the first day of September; he returned to Lancashire in the following year.

The administration of the Hunt was by 1833 in the hands of a group which then took the lease of newly built Hunt Kennels near East Hardwick: Hon E W Harvey, fourth Lord Hawke, Womersley Hall; Sir F L Wood, baronet, Hickleton Hall; Robert Oliver, Darrington Hall; Joseph Scott, Badsworth Hall; George Greaves, Elmsall Lodge; Godfrey Wentworth, Woolley Hall; John Gully, Ackworth Park; Philip Davies Cooke, Owston Hall; Joseph Copley, Sprotborough Hall

The new kennels of 1833 had then been recently built by John Richards, the Badsworth's own Huntsman (who died in 1835), on land he purchased in 1828; previously they had been in nearby Thorpe Audlin, from whence he came. The new kennels were bought in 1859 to form part of the Ackworth Grange estate of the Tempest family and were used until 1954 when the Badsworth kennels were moved to the again nearby mansion Hillthorpe, bought by the Hunt, where modern accommodation for hounds, horses and hunt staff was provided.

When the surviving committee minutes of the Hunt begin, in 1876, the Hunt committee so-called consisted of J H Barton, Master, of Stapleton Park; R T Lee, Grove Hall, Knottingley; J C D C Charlesworth, Chapelthorpe Hall, near Wakefield; and Sir L M S Pilkington, baronet, Chevet Hall, Wakefield.

There was a debit balance against the Hunt in 1876 of over £450; the accounts for the year 1875-6 show expenditure totalling £3,324 5s 6d, plus, of course the adverse balance, while subscriptions totalled only £2,598 11s 6d. At that time, Sir Lionel M S Pilkington was honorary secretary of the Hunt committee. All the way through from 1869 to 1875 expenditure had considerably outstripped income. The expenditures of 1875-6 are listed as:

	£	s	d
purchase of horses	493	10	
hay, corn, straw and beans	384	14	3
oatmeal and biscuit	785	17	9
flesh	150	19	6
kennel and cottage rents	143	15	10
taxes and licences	44	16	8
clothing	52	5	2
coals and leading them	84	5	8
blacksmith, chemist, saddler etc	120	13	11
wages	602	18	5
carriages, postages, railway fares and stationery	70	7	5
repairs - carpenter, mason, plumber	77	14	6
cover rents	15	9	0
bank interest	21	5	8
interest on bonds etc	24	0	0

By the year 1890-91 subscriptions were lower in total than fifteen years earlier, at £2,273 3s 6d; there were now eleven committee members (and subsequently between seven and twelve), and 118 subscriptions including those of five females, all ranging between one guinea and £100. Although in the 1890s the committee was composed entirely of gentry, some of them were commercial men and included two still-working colliery owners, a banker and a soap manufacturer. The membership of the Hunt extended geographically

Figure 8. The old Bay Horse and bridge, Wentbridge, sketched by G Percy Rhodes for 'Memorials of a Yorkshire Parish', J S Fletcher (1914).

from Brighouse, Huddersfield and Halifax in the west to Doncaster in the east, and from Bradford in the north to Sheffield in the south. It included peers – the Earl of Mexborough of Methley Park, Lord St Oswald of Nostell and Lord Houghton of Fryston Hall, through titled and landed gentry and army officers, to tradesmen – to the owner of the *Wakefield Express* newspaper, a Wakefield vet, and a surveyor there, and E W Glover the Wakefield auctioneer. Indeed over sixteen per cent of the membership came from the vicinity of Wakefield, with further considerable percentages from the Doncaster, Pontefract and even Barnsley areas too. The annual income of the Hunt in fact varied considerably, and it had risen to £2,835 in 1897-98.

The Hunt had a social aspect too, beyond the socializing at Hunt meetings. The third Earl of Darlington (1766-1842), who became first Duke of Cleveland in 1833, owned Bilham House near Hooton Pagnall, and brought his hounds from his Raby Castle in County Durham to the Badsworth country while establishing the Badsworth Hunt Club at Ferrybridge, then, of course, an important coaching town, while the Bay Horse Inn at Wentbridge was the home of the annual Fox Feasts, given by the Hunt committee to all the gamekeepers employed at the country estates in the area (Figure 8).

The day-to-day activities of the Victorian Hunt, its meets which were, after all, its sole real concern, are recorded in some detail in the surviving diaries of Edward Simpson (1843-1894) of Walton near Wakefield. He was a man of considerable opulence until his fall from financial grace in the first years of the twentieth century. Briefly, he was the son of an illegitimate man who had been admitted as a manufacturer to a small established business run by his probable father, in 1833, and who died in 1873 leaving effects valued at some £250,000. The son, intended initially for the church, joined the family business along with his brother; he became additionally a colliery owner and a director of the local Wakefield and Barnsley Union Bank, and was able to lay out £114,000 upon the purchase of the Walton Hall estate in 1877 – a huge sum although one inflated by the supposed value of what turned out to be then unworkable coal resources. Edward Simpson's voluminous surviving papers illustrate his many interests in local life, and show him as a hard and ambitious man, although one apparently really devoted to hunting. From 1891 he was able to live at Walton Hall, previously leased out, and he was a magistrate locally. He was a member of the committee of the Badsworth Hunt, although, of course, a hunt committee merely represented the interests of the subscribers and elected a Master, who has been described as always a 'sort of dictator', holding office for a year and receiving by far the largest proportion of the subscription income from the Hunt and the loan of hounds and kennels, agreeing in return to hunt on the days laid down by the committee and to bear almost the whole of the costs of doing so himself, in large part from subscription monies paid over to him. Edward Simpson served on the Badsworth Hunt committee throughout the 1890s and subscribed a substantial £50 a year to the Hunt.

Simpson's diary for 1874 may be taken as typical. In February the Hunt meets at Ackworth Moor Top:

Tried Taylor Wood & all Nostell but as it was wet and rough he came home (Figure 9).

Two days later the Hunt met at Hemsworth:

Got on the trail of a fox at Hugg Wood but made nothing out, drew

Figure 9. The *Boot and Shoe*, Ackworth in 2001. In the nineteenth century it was a regular meeting place for the Badsworth Hunt. *Kate Taylor.*

Vissitt & Sir Lionel's [Pilkington's] *Gorses blank then went to Day's Cover where we left.*

Early in March the meet was at Wentbridge and a vixen was found at Brocadale:

Found in Stapleton, across [River] *Went to Stapleton, then to Barnsdale, Kirk Smeaton and again across the Went towards Norton*

where he left. A portion of his diary shows how regularly he hunted:

19 March 1874	*meet at Darrington*
21 March	*meet at Brierley - found a fox*
24 March	*meet at High Melton village, found near Melton Hall*
26 March	*meet Womersley*
28 March	*meet Notton: three foxes found*

In August 1874 the hounds began cub hunting, and continued through September.

Simpson's other papers record interesting aspects of the Hunt: in 1893 he was corresponding in regard to the supply to the Badsworth of fifty fox-cubs and grown ones, at a cost of £57 15s, discussing a supply from Scotland – foxes were being brought in to the Hunt country in considerable numbers. The Hunt's Poultry Fund, which recompensed poultry owners from losses occasioned by foxes, shows payment made of between 12s 6d to £3 to poultry owners in a wide area covered by the Hunt: Gunthwaite near Penistone, Silkstone, Clayton West, Holme, Flockton, Bolton on Dearne, Emley, Cawthorne, Coxley Valley, Middlestown, and towards Barnsley, Doncaster and Fishlake.

Edward Simpson himself would go hunting in North Lincolnshire in the 1870s and early in 1896 he was organizing a special train to take the Hunt, along with the hounds and the horses, to Brocklesby for the day. In 1901 he organized a cricket match between the Badsworth and the Bramham Moor Hunts' teams, and in 1908 he received a list of the young new hounds, the Young Entry, with their individual names, sire, dam, date whelped and by whom walked, ie what farms they were kept on. In 1894 he deals with mange in the foxes: the fox earths were to be cleaned out.

In 1892 C B E Wright JP, DL, son of Bilham House near Doncaster and Bolton Hall near Clitheroe, left the Badsworth after sixteen seasons (or years) as its Master, to go to manage the Milton Kennels near Peterborough. He had done wonders for the Badsworth: he was a great hound man, the blood of the Badsworth hounds being sought after by other kennel breeders, hunting himself and mounting himself and the Hunt's servants on the best of horses. Edward Simpson was involved in the presentation to Wright of his portrait, at a cost of £238 6s. Then came the three-season reign of Lt Col W J F Ramsden JP, of the Coldstream Guards, born in 1845 and resident at Rogerthorpe Manor, Badsworth, and upon his leaving in 1895, Simpson, as one of the Hunt committee, was involved in the appointment of a new Master. The committee met at the Kennels to consider applications. Edward Simpson was asked would S D Price-Davies of Chirbury, Shropshire, who had married a daughter of the Charlesworth colliery-owning family of Wakefield, suit as Master, or perhaps Peake, who had offered to spend £1,000 a year 'on the job'? In the event the choice fell upon John Fullerton JP, DL, born in 1865 and hence a man of only some thirty, of the huge Thrybergh Park near Rotherham, who held the office of Master very successfully for seven years. When Wright had come as Master in 1876 he had agreed to leave the hounds, when he went, in quality and number as he had found them, taking over fifty-two of the fifty-six and a half couples (113 hounds in all) then belonging to the Hunt.

And so, something of the earlier story of the great Badsworth Hunt and of a very few of those persons and places associated with it. That the Hunt changed, not only – and obviously – in its personnel in this period, but changed too in its social structure, its method of financing, and in its organization, is apparent, but throughout it continued to provide excitement, exercise and a socializing facility as between the upper and middle classes, and, to a degree, as suggested by William Whiteley's experiences with it, for some of the farming class too.

Sources

Printed
H Clarkson et al, Badsworth Hunt Country map, 1826.
H Clarkson, *Memories of Merry Wakefield*, 1st edition, 1887.
R S Lambert, *The Universal Provider, William Whiteley*, 1938.
T W Tew, *Miscellaneous Papers*, 1892.
A P W Stirling, *Annals of a Yorkshire House*, 2 vols.
W Scarth-Dixon, *The Badsworth*, 1921-22.
Anon, *Hunting in Yorkshire*, new edition, no date.
Memoirs of the late Mrs Catherine Cappe, 1822.
Burke's Landed Gentry and *Peerage*, various editions of each.
Sale plans and particulars.

Manuscript
John Goodchild's Local History Study Centre, Wakefield: Aldam mss; Hodgson and Simpson mss; Registry of Deeds mss; Newland mss; Micklethwait of Painthorpe mss; Ackworth Grange mss; William Pease of Pontefract account book.
Badsworth Hunt mss, in the custody of its joint honorary secretary.
Reverend James Torre ledger, in private ownership.
Oral information from Mr Gordon Smith, Doncaster.

4. Of Graves and Epitaphs: Wakefield Cemetery

by Anthony Petyt

MOST OF WAKEFIELD'S OLDER RESIDENTS will know well the cemetery on Doncaster Road (Figure 1).

They will remember the sad occasions of the funerals of family and friends and also subsequent visits to lay flowers on the graves. In Victorian times the visiting of the graves of relatives was a popular Sunday pastime, however, very few of these visitors would have given a thought to the reasons why their loved ones were buried in a municipal cemetery rather than the traditional graveyard of a parish church.

The industrial revolution brought about a rapid increase in the populations of towns as agricultural labourers abandoned the land in search of better paid jobs in the factories. Coupled with this was a general increase in the population. For the first time the births outnumbered the deaths. In England and Wales the population rose from 9,000,000 in 1800 to 32,500,000 at the end of the century.[1] This led to inadequate housing conditions in the towns and also to great pressure on the primitive water supply and sewerage systems.

Figure 1. A general view of Wakefield Cemetery. *Anthony Petyt.*

Another problem facing the authorities was the dreadful state of the burial grounds within the towns. At the start of the nineteenth century the only available means of disposing of the dead was by burial. Every person had a common-law right to be buried in the churchyard of the parish where they died and relatives could claim that right for those who died outside their own parish. People did claim their rights and as a result most town-centre burial ground sbecame full to overflowing and in a deplorable condition. Wakefield was no exception but of course its problems were not as great as its larger neighbours such as Leeds and Bradford.

By the early 1800s the graveyard surrounding the parish church was full and for some years Vicarage Croft, a piece of land adjoining the Rectory and Vicarage Houses, had been used, through the permission of the different vicars, as an additional burial ground. On 22 January, 1815 this ground was conveyed by the Reverend Samuel Sharp, the then Vicar to certain Trustees for the use of the inhabitants of Wakefield as a burial ground. The Archbishop of York later consecrated the ground.[2] There were other places of burial in the town. There was a graveyard surrounding Thornes Church which is still in use at the present day. The Unitarians had a graveyard on Westgate, the Methodists on Thornhill Street and there was a small burial ground by the side of Zion Chapel on George Street.

In the late 1840s the burial ground belonging to Wakefield parish church was full. This was apparent to the church authorities and they started discussions either for an extension to the existing burial ground or the provision of a new one on another site. As is usual, with anything new or different, opinions differed and the arguments raged, sometimes being conducted in the local newspaper. In March 1850, Dr William Wood, chairman of the churchwardens, wrote to the editor of the *Wakefield Journal* denying that the churchwardens had ever recommended a site for a new burial ground outside the parish. However he admitted they had been offered two pieces of land in the parish of Sandal which were at once declined. This is ironic because the new cemetery was eventually situated in Sandal but by then the matter had been taken out of the hands of the church.

Burial Acts relating to London were passed in 1850 and 1852 banning further burials in churches and churchyards in the metropolis other than in family graves. London parishes were empowered, but not obliged, to appoint burial boards to make arrangements for burying the dead. They could either contract with the existing commercial cemeteries, or start their own, using money from the Poor Rate or else borrow money to make purchases of suitable land. In 1853 the arrangements of the *Metropolitan Burial Act* for London were extended to the rest of England and Wales. The Secretary of State was given power to prohibit further burials in any given place in England and Wales and provisions were made for establishing new public cemeteries by means of Parochial Burial Boards.[3]

Remembering the outbreak of cholera in 1849, when 87 people had died, the Wakefield Town Council petitioned the Board of Health to apply the *Public Health Act* of 1847 to the borough and to empower the Council to act as a Local Board of Health. These powers, if granted, would give the borough increased authority for services such as water and drainage and enable them to establish a borough cemetery. In 1851, a Board of Health Inspector, William Ranger, conducted an inquiry into the 'sewerage drainage and supply of water, and the sanitary conditions of the inhabitants of Wakefield'.[4] His enquiry was thorough and far-reaching. On the subject of burial he questioned very closely those in charge of the churches and chapels with burial grounds. Naturally these denied that there was a problem but the questions posed by Mr Ranger suggested otherwise. Oral evidence revealed a dreadful situation. Sextons reported that when opening graves for burials they often exposed coffins and bones which had to be hidden from mourners until after the funeral and then re-interred. Vicarage Croft, the graveyard of the parish church, was said to be 'overcrowded and in a very unhealthy state' and 'Wrengate , in the immediate vicinity was the constant seat of fever'. Many witnesses advocated the provision of a single, general cemetery. William Ranger agreed and in his report he stated that 'no time should be lost in the formation of a general cemetery'.

It took the Borough Council another six years to make a decision but in October 1857 the Council bought Sir Lionel Pilkington's Belle Vue estate for £5,500.[5] A Burial Board was formed soon after. It was always intended that the local authority rather than a commercial company should administer the cemetery at Wakefield. In London private companies had established many cemeteries such as those at Highgate and Kensal Green whilst in Yorkshire private enterprise had provided cemeteries at Woodhouse in Leeds and Undercliffe at Bradford. By March the following year the Board had approved the design for twin chapels –one for the established church and one for dissenters (Figure 2). These plans were prepared by M O Tarbotton, the Borough Surveyor and the buildings erected by

Figure 2. The twin chapels, now demolished. *Anthony Petyt.*

Barton, Son and Moulson at a cost of £1,678. The Council also paid a local nurseryman, William Barratt of St John's, £98 to plant trees and shrubs. A lodge was built at the Doncaster Road entrance for the Registrar and Curator (Figure 3). Thomas Amys was appointed to this position at a salary of £75 plus the house free of rent and rates. The cemetery, which was twenty acres in size, was divided into two parts, one for dissenters and the other for the established Church. Originally the section to the right of the chapels when entering the cemetery from Sugar Lane was reserved for the Church of England burials whilst the section to the left was used by the nonconformists with the Roman Catholics being buried usually along the wall side of Sugar Lane. Over the years, due to the pressure on space, these divisions have become blurred and in today's world when we live in a multicultural society with many religions, clergymen tend to consecrate individual graves rather than whole sections of the

Figure 3. The lodge at the Doncaster Road entrance to the cemetery..

Figure 4. Monuments ranging from the simple to the grand. *Anthony Petyt.*

graveyard. This is especially the case in the new lawn cemetery in Sugar Lane which was opened in 1961.

The first burial in the cemetery took place, by special permission of the Burial Board Committee, in the non-conformist area on 13 April, 1859 when Mrs. Henry Lee, wife of Councillor Lee of Burton Street was interred. A service, conducted by the Reverend John Shepherd Eastmead, had been held at Salem Chapel, Wakefield before proceeding to the cemetery. A report in the *Wakefield Express*, three days later, described the funeral and went on to say that it was hoped a part of the cemetery would be consecrated in six to eight weeks after which it would be finally opened. The report added 'We understand that the Borough Surveyor is now engaged in marking the spaces to be devoted to the purposes of sepulture'. On 18 June, 1859, the Bishop of Ripon conducted a service of consecration and all was ready at long last.

Wakefield cemetery caters for all sections of the community and its monuments range from the simple to the very grand (Figure 4). The largest, but certainly not the grandest, is that erected over the grave of William Shaw, builder and engineering contractor, who died in November 1859. In other parts of the cemetery, apart from the usual type of tombstone, there is a good selection of obelisks, broken columns, anchors, open books, draped urns and a great variety of crosses. In the Catholic section you will find representations of Christ and the Madonna. Several are complete with elaborate sculptures such as angels, which were, perhaps, erected to impress the living rather than to commemorate the dead. Most of the memorials would be carved by local craftsmen, especially in an area like West Yorkshire where there was a good supply of stone from local

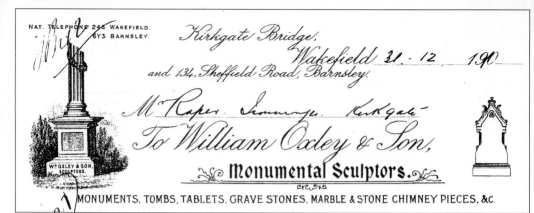

Figure 5. Bill-head of 1910 for the firm of William Oxley, monumental sculptors.

quarries (Figures 5 and 6). If you wanted a marble angel it usually had to be chosen from a catalogue of imported monuments. Most of these imports came from Italy where the masons were thought to be superior in their handling of the human figure. The advent of the railways and the improvement of other forms of transport would have eased the importation of such items.

Scattered throughout the cemetery are several stones provided by the War Graves Commission to honour the dead of two world wars.

Strangely there seem to be very few verses on the gravestones. Perhaps by the middle of the nineteenth century that kind of sentimentality was considered old-fashioned or was it that the hard working folk of Wakefield were reluctant to express their feelings in such a public way? There are however, what today would be called one-liners. There are the very short statements: *Gone Home, At Rest, Thy Will Be Done, Deeply Regretted,* or *Affectionate Remembrance.* Some express resignation – *Where We Live We Die, Thy Will Lord, Not Mine,* and *Our Lives Were In God's Hands.* Others are more hopeful – *At Rest Until The Day Dawns, Rest Well Brave Heart* and the popular *Not Lost But Gone Before.* On children's graves the sorrowing parents sometimes felt they could express themselves more freely with such sentiments as *A Sweet And Lovely Gem Entered The Saviour's Kingdom,* and *Suffer Little Children To Come Unto Me.*

Figure 6. Bill-head for a Wakefield undertaker.

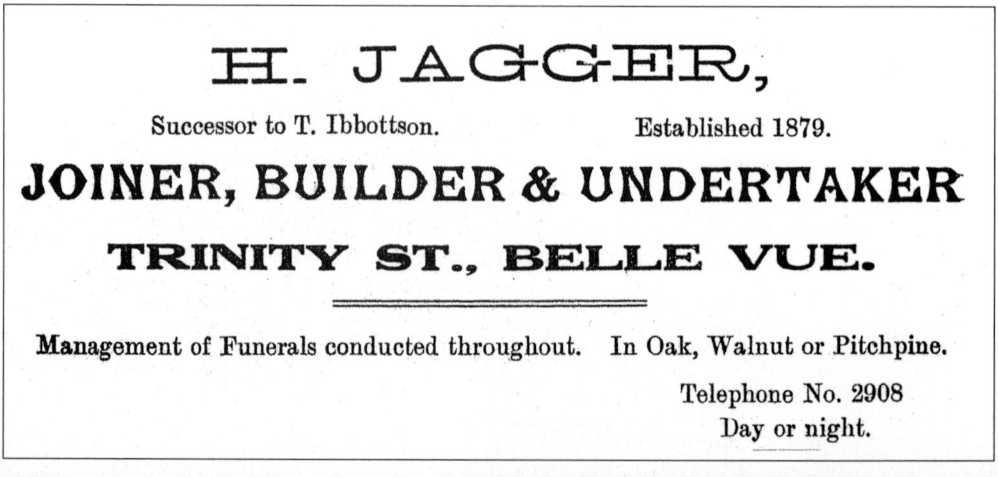

Over the last thirty or so years Wakefield has suffered from the modern curse of vandalism. In May 1970 the *Wakefield Express* reported that twenty graves had been damaged and desecrated and the damage amounted to about £1,100. The paper dubbed the vandals 'Moonlight Marauders' but Councillor Sutcliffe was probably more accurate when he said, 'We are dealing with madmen... this is not the work of children'. Damage to individual monuments and to the twin chapels continued in spite of valiant work done by the police and the cemetery staff, although Wakefield suffered less than other places. In February 1991 a Council sub-committee was told that the chapels had not been used for ten years and they were in a very poor state of repair. Officers were asked to investigate their possible future use. The following month the chapels were set on fire by vandals and damage was caused amounting to £50,000. At a meeting in May 1991 the Council were told the chapels were in so poor a state that it would cost £140,000 to repair them. In view of the enormous cost it was decided to demolish them but to preserve the central tower. The lodge at the Doncaster Road entrance is still standing but is no longer inhabited by a member of the cemetery staff. The vandalism seems to be on the wane; at the present time the cemetery is in good condition and well looked after by the Council.

Since the cemetery opened in 1859 over 66,000 burials have taken place but it is interesting to note that since 1961 when the crematorium was built at Kettlethorpe over 32,000 cremations have taken place in Wakefield (Figure 7). Wakefield was rather late in getting its own crematorium and prior to 1961 Wakefield people who preferred cremation had to use the crematoria in Leeds. It is obvious

Figure 7. Wakefield Crematorium, Kettlethorpe, in 2001. *Kate Taylor.*

the demand for burials has decreased. Since its first controversial beginnings in the 1880s, cremation has grown steadily: something between sixty per cent and seventy per cent of all funerals now involve cremation rather than burial.

Most of the people buried in the cemetery are the ordinary working folk of Wakefield. As in most provincial towns anybody who achieved national or international fame often left the area and was buried elsewhere. Of course many talented people stayed in Wakefield and they contributed to the prosperity of the town. These included the woollen manufacturers, engineers, colliery proprietors, corn merchants, maltsters and brewers and the like. There were also the professional classes such as lawyers, clergymen and doctors. Another important group comprised the local politicians and the people employed to run local services. Many of these people are buried in the cemetery, the more prosperous of them are under the larger monuments grouped around the chapels.

On entering the cemetery through the Doncaster Road entrance one of the first things to be seen is the very tall obelisk erected to the memory of William Harrison, first Mayor of Wakefield, who died in 1860. A closer inspection of the inscription reveals that this monument

> *was erected by subscription as a tribute of respect to the private worth and public spirit of the late George William Harrison Esq. He was the first Mayor of this borough and was twice elected to that office.*

This is not a grave as the inscription goes on to say that Mr. Harrison died at Malvern and was buried in his family's burial ground at Scagglethorpe near Malton.

There are several other former Mayors of Wakefield buried in the cemetery. These include George Blakeley who died in 1922 and William Rhodes who died during his year of office in 1904.[6] Mr. Rhodes was the owner of Grove Iron Works and the son of Joseph Rhodes who was also Mayor of Wakefield. His obituary in the *Wakefield Express* fills a full page and his monument in the cemetery is also on a very large scale. It comprises a plinth of about six feet in height surmounted by a similarly sized angel complete with wings. The whole monument is of a very white stone which has weathered well over the years (Figure 8). Not far from this grave is the family plot of the Mackie family who were of Scottish origin and were corn merchants. They took an interest in the town, were involved in local politics and were generous benefactors to many causes. Robert Bownas Mackie was the Liberal Member of Parliament for Wakefield from 1880 until his death in 1885.

Not far from the site of the chapels is the grave of Thomas Clayton (Figure 9). This name is known to most citizens of Wakefield as one of the main benefactors of the hospital which now bears his name. He was born in Wakefield in 1786, the son of a tallow chandler. The business was such a success that both father and son were able to retire in 1826 and Thomas devoted the rest of his life to public work and philanthropy. In 1850 he was elected as an Alderman and in 1854 became Mayor. It was in this year that Clayton gave the first of his donations towards the provision of hospital facilities in Wakefield. He gave £824 for the purchase of the premises then rented by the Wakefield Dispensary off Northgate. In 1860 he gave another donation of £150 to complete the premises. Between these two dates the institution altered its name to the Clayton Hospital and Wakefield General

Figure 8. The monument to William Rhodes, a former mayor of Wakefield, who died in 1904. *Anthony Petyt.*

Dispensary. Many other generous gifts of money were made over the years and when Thomas Clayton died in 1868 he left the hospital a legacy of £300 per year. Over the years the hospital became too small for the needs of a quickly growing town and in 1879 the new building was opened on its present site on Northgate.[7]

On the other side of the chapels in the consecrated part of the cemetery lies another doctor well known to many not for his medical

Figure 9. The grave of Thomas Clayton. *Anthony Petyt.*

skills but for his talent as an artist. Dr Henry Clarke came to Wakefield in 1876 to take up the post of surgeon at Wakefield Prison.[8] He had been born in Middlesex, studied medicine at Durham and for two years was acting house surgeon at Guy's Hospital in London. Dr Clarke worked diligently at his job at the prison and in his spare time set about recording the Wakefield of his day in the form of almost one hundred drawings. These drawings were bound into a copy of Henry Clarkson's *Memories of Merry Wakefield* and were later bequeathed by Dr Clarke's daughter, Gladys Clarke, to the Wakefield Corporation in 1960. The Wakefield Historical Society published a collection of these drawings in 1977. Dr Clarke retired from the Prison Service in 1908; he spent the remainder of his life at High Wycombe in Buckinghamshire and when he died aged seventy-two in1920 he was brought back to Wakefield to be buried with his wife Louisa.[9]

Figure 10. Thomas Waller Gissing, father of the novelist, George Gissing.

Further down the cemetery lie the remains of another prison doctor. This is William R Milner, *Twenty years resident surgeon to the convict department of the West Riding House of Correction, born 1810, died 17 August, 1868.* In the next grave lies a friend of Dr Milner, who, whilst not a medical man, was connected with the health of the public. This was Thomas Waller Gissing, a pharmaceutical chemist, a botanist and poet (Figure 10). Gissing was a Suffolk man and after training as a pharmacist came to Wakefield to open his own business at the top of Westgate. He combined the running of his business with public work. He was a local councillor, librarian at the Mechanics Institution and a member of many other organisations. Before coming to Wakefield he had published three books of poetry and during his time in Wakefield wrote two books about the natural history of the area. He led a very busy life and it was probably overwork that led to his early death in 1870. His main claim to fame is that he was the father of the highly regarded Victorian novelist, George Gissing, whose life and works are celebrated in the Gissing Centre which has been established in his birthplace in Thompson's Yard at the top of Westgate.

Most Church of England clergymen are buried in graveyards attached to parish churches. An exception is the Reverend Charles Joseph Camidge MA who was Vicar of Wakefield from 1855 to

1875.[10] He was the last vicar to reside in the old Vicarage House, which after the institution of his successor, Reverend Norman Straton, was purchased by Sir Edward Green, and in 1876 was opened as a Conservative club.

In the unconsecrated section is a very large monument, about eight feet high and topped with a draped urn. This marks the grave of the Reverend Harvey Leigh, a Primitive Methodist Minister, who died in 1878. He had worked in the Wakefield and Barnsley areas for over thirty-nine years. His son, the Reverend William Bramwell Leigh is also buried in this grave. Also interred in this section is the Reverend John Shepherd Eastmead, who it will be remembered, conducted the first burial in the cemetery in 1859. His gravestone tells us the he was '30 years Minister of Salem Chapel, Wakefield and that he died Sunday evening, 11 October, 1885'. Not far away in an area devoted to Roman Catholics is a large burial plot containing the remains of six priests who served at St Austin's Church. Amongst them is the much loved Monseigneur Henry Thompson who was parish priest at St Austin's for forty-two years and died in 1991 aged eighty-seven years.

The legal profession is well represented by solicitors, barristers and Justices of the Peace. Someone like Samuel Bruce was both barrister and a J P. An interesting case is that of James Whitham who was a solicitor and also the Town Clerk of Wakefield. He was born in Bangalore in 1812 and came to England in 1817. As a young man he was articled to William Pickard of Barstow Square, who was known as the 'honest blind lawyer' and he later succeeded to the business. Whitham died in 1867.[11]

The only titled person I can find in the cemetery was also a solicitor by training. He was Sir Charles McGrath and his gravestone tells us that 'he was sometime clerk of the peace and of the County Council of the W R of Yorkshire'. McGrath started his career in a solicitor's office in Skipton and by hard work and ability achieved great eminence in public administration for which he was knighted in 1933. At the beginning of the second world war, Sir Charles, at the request of the War Office, raised the Wakefield Medium Battery of Artillery, which gave distinguished service at Dunkirk. He was also appointed Deputy Regional Commissioner for Civil Defence, a post he held from 1939 to 1941, but he upset Whitehall by saying in public, 'We will not bring Hitler to his knees by sand bagging public buildings' and that 'the nation's prime duty is to concentrate on the line-up of a first class fighting force'. Sir Charles died aged eighty in 1951 at his home, Stanley Grange.[12]

No doubt there are many policemen buried in the cemetery. There are three from the early days of the Wakefield Force. In the Catholic section lies James McDonald, 'late Chief Constable of Wakefield, died June 21 1868 aged fifty-four'. His obituary in the *Wakefield Express* stated that he had been Chief Constable ever since the incorporation of the borough in 1848. Apparently he 'took cold' after a fishing excursion and this was followed by rheumatic fever.[13] The report goes on to say that he 'leaves a large family to deplore his loss'. His funeral was attended by the Mayor and most of the corporation. Two other gravestones tell us that Superintendent John Royston of the Borough Police, Wakefield, died in 1869 and that Charles Perkin, fifteen years a Constable in the Wakefield Borough Police Force died in 1875.

Many other tombstones tell us about the deceased's trade or calling. Most of these are what you would expect to find in Wakefield such as Joseph Milsom, Engineer of this town, died 1869; John Bairstow, Worsted Spinner, died 1916; James Hodgson, Stuff Merchant of Kirkgate, died 1859; Sam Storr, Builder and Contractor, died 1899; Edward Turner, Engine Driver, died 1865 and James Craven, Boat Builder of Wakefield. Died 1882. Then there are more unusual trades such as that followed by George Parkin who died in 1879, who was a gravestone letterer. There is the more refined trade followed by Thomas Edmund Grace who died in 1876 (and worked for his father), John, who was a Carver, Gilder and Fine Art Dealer. And who would expect to find the following gravestone in the cemetery of an industrial town,

> *Edwin Owen, Whipper-in and Huntsman to the Badsworth Hounds for more than 25 years. Died September 25 1877 aged 58. Erected by a few friends as a memorial of respect and esteem.*

Wakefield has always been renowned for the large number of public houses in the town and as a consequence there are several innkeepers buried in the cemetery. Curiously, the families of deceased publicans seemed to like verses on their tombstones as in the case of Philip Mayman of Wakefield, Innkeeper who died in 1862.

> *A better husband never lived,*
> *A kinder father never died,*
> *His honest heart no man deceived,*
> *His manly spirit knew no pride.*
> *His memory fondly in our hearts shall rest,*
> *And as on earth in heaven for ever blest.*

Other landlords include James Edgar of the *College Hotel*, Northgate, who died in 1886, Joseph Cliff formerly of the *White Swan Inn*, Kirkgate who passed away in 1883 and James Crabtree of the *Castle Inn*, Sandal who was buried in the cemetery in 1896. Innkeepers need suppliers and in other parts of the cemetery you will find the tall obelisk which marks the grave of the Ash family, maltsters of Wakefield and the equally impressive monument to the Beverley family, brewers, maltsters and wine merchants.

Most people hope to die in their own beds of old age but as some gravestones tell us this is not always the case. In the case of children it is particularly sad. The gravestone of William Smith states that he was drowned whilst bathing in the river Calder on 28 June, 1863 in his fourteenth year. Not far away is the grave of poor John Willie Sykes who was accidentally drowned 12 August, 1877 aged seven years.[14] An inquest held at the *Ship Inn* informs us that he was the son of James Sykes of Gibson's Yard, Kirkgate and that he, along with other boys went to bathe in the river opposite Mr Green's works. It seems that he got out of his depth and disappeared beneath the water. Henry Abell, a cooper, jumped into the river in an attempt to save him but was unsuccessful. Another sad case of the death of a child is that of Mary Elizabeth Gilbert who died in 1869. According to a report in the *Wakefield Express* she was sent to look for her brother who was playing with friends at 'Rantipole' on a pile of planks in Wagon Warehouse Yard, Westgate. Apparently the pile of planks collapsed completely burying the girl. Workers from the nearby works of Messrs Teall rushed to the scene and removed the planks but Mary was found to be dead.[15]

In past times accidents at work were quite common. Walter Hudson's gravestone tells us that he was accidentally killed at the Church Congress Hall, Wakefield on 15 October, 1866. An inquest was told that he was engaged in taking down scaffolding at the Corn Exchange where the Church Congress of 1866 had been held. An iron bar snapped and he fell thirty feet to the floor and died later from his injuries. He left a widow and eight children.[16] The Bishop of Ripon wrote to *The Times* asking those who had attended the Church Congress to contribute to an appeal that was being organised by the Vicar of St Andrew's Church. Another works accident was that of George Brosker, a goods guard on the railway who was killed at Hemsworth. His gravestone has a verse carved on it which poses a question which can only have one answer.

Sudden was the death of me and great surprise to all,
When God did say I must go away could I refuse the call?

Surprisingly for an inland town there are two deaths of seamen recorded in the cemetery. Charles Anakin, mariner of Hull, died at Singapore in 1865. The stone was erected by his widow, Rhoda, who died in Wakefield in 1879. On a stone decorated with a beautiful carving of a fully rigged ship is recorded the death of George Lindley who was lost at sea in the ship *Royal Albert* in 1866 (Figure 11). In an account of shipping disasters in *The Times* of 18 January 1866 it is reported that

Figure 11. The grave of George Lindley who died in 1866. *Anthony Petyt.*

the ship Royal Albert under Captain Davis and belonging to Messrs Fernie of Liverpool, sailed from Calcutta to London on 19 September last with a cargo of cotton, tea, jute and seeds. She appears to have been lost near Bude and a large part of the cargo, the Captain's desk and one of the lifebuoys had been washed ashore. [17]

There are other instances of deaths occurring overseas and being recorded on the family gravestone. These may have been cases of young men going to America or the Colonies to start a new life or possibly like William Lee, who died at Rheinfelder in Switzerland in 1891, were on holiday or travelling to a healthier climate. Matthew Hick, who was the son of Matthew Bussey Hick of Chald House, Westgate, was sent to Australia by his father after a series of indiscretions in Wakefield. He died in Melbourne in 1886. Charles Edward Petty, the son of a general labourer, was a bright boy who in 1881 was a clerk in the Town Clerk's office in Wakefield. Perhaps he thought that he had better prospects in America, but it was not to be. He died at the early age of twenty-four and is buried in the cemetery at Evanstone in Wyoming.

Some graves stand out because they have unusual carvings or their occupants have unusual names. Examples of the latter would be Cinderella Wilson who died in 1891; Onesimus Riley, a grocer's manager who died in 1904 and Aquilla Morley, a coal miner who died in 1915. Catherine Otway, who was the wife of a Staff Captain in the Salvation Army, has a gravestone beautifully carved with the insignia of the Salvation Army. William Fawsitt, who died in 1863,

WAKEFIELD CITY BURIAL GROUND.

REGISTER OF GRANTS No. 1836

We, the Mayor, Aldermen and Citizens of the City of Wakefield, in the County of York, in consideration of the sum of _One Pound_ ————————————————————— Paid by _Susan Jane Morley, Widow, of 95 Quaker House Yard, Belle Vue, Wakefield, and of Oliv Hiscock, Married Woman, of 6 Castle Terrace, Walton, Wakefield_ —— in the County of York ——————————————— the receipt whereof is hereby acknowledged Do, by virtue of the powers vested in us by the Acts of 15 and 16 Victoria, chapter 85, and 16 and 17 Victoria, chapter 134 hereby grant unto the said _Susan Jane Morley and Oliv Hiscock_ the exclusive Right of Burial in all that Freehold Grave Plot Numbered ——— _610_ ——— in Section— _L_ —— on the Plan of the Burial Ground, made in pursuance of the said Acts, being part of the Burial Ground provided under the said Acts by the Mayor, Aldermen and Citizens aforesaid, To hold the same to the said _Susan Jane Morley and Oliv Hiscock_ ——— their respective Heirs and Assigns, for ever, for the purpose of Burial Subject nevertheless to the Payment of such Fees or Sums as are reserved by the said Acts, and to the Rules and Regulations for the time being affecting the said Burial Ground.

Given under the Corporate Common Seal of the City of Wakefield, this _Twenty pisth_ —— day of_ June ——— One Thousand Nine Hundred and Thirty six ————

The Common Seal of the Mayor, Aldermen and
Citizens of the City of Wakefield was
hereunto duly affixed in the presence of

Town Clerk.

Figure 12. Certificate showing the sale in 1936 of the right of burial in a plot at Wakefield Cemetery.

whose gravestone is decorated with a square and compass, was obviously a Freemason. Another stone has a carving of shaking hands and has the inscription

> Erected by the members of the Wakefield and District Ancient Order of Foresters as a memento of respect to the late brother Thomas Whitehead of Northgate, 16 years their Treasurer, died September 24th 1876.

It is difficult to predict what the future holds for Victorian cemeteries. With the passing of time there will be fewer relatives to visit the graves and take an interest in the general upkeep of the cemeteries (Figure 12). There are, however, groups of people, such as local historians and genealogists, who are keen to see these places preserved but are they prepared to bear the costs?

Notes and References

1. Chris Brooks, *Mortal Remains*, 1989, page 1.
2. Rev. J L Sissons, *Historic Sketch of the Parish Church of Wakefield*, 1824, page 71.
3. Chris Brooks, *Mortal Remains*, 1989, page 48.
4. William Ranger, Report to the General Board of Health on a preliminary inquiry into the sewerage, drainage and supply of water and the sanitary condition of the inhabitants of Wakefield, 1852.
5. *Wakefield Express*, 5 September 1857, page 3.
6. *Ibid.* 21 May 1904, page 10.
7. *Ibid*, 24 October 1868, page 5.
8. Henry Clarke, *Drawings of Wakefield*, 1977.
9. *Wakefield Express*, 16 October 1920, page 11.
10. *Ibid*, 11 July 1875, page 5.
11. *Ibid*, 27 April 1867, page 8.
12. *Ibid*, 17 February 1951, page 8.
13. *Ibid*, 27 June 1868, page 5.
14. *Ibid*, 18 August 1877, page 5.
15. *Ibid*, 14 August 1869, page 4.
16. *Ibid*, 23 October 1866, page 5.
17. *The Times*, 18 January 1866, page 9.

Sources

1. Sylvia M Barnard, *To Prove I'm Not Forgot*, 1990.
2. Alfred Fellows, *The Law of Burial*, 1952.
3. James Stevens Curl, *The Victorian Celebration of Death*, 1972.
4. Chris Brooks, *Mortal Remains*, 1989.
5. David Robinson & Dean Koontz, *Beautiful Death – Art of the Cemetery*, 1996.
6. Wakefield M D C, *Cemeteries and Crematoria*, 1996.
7. J W Walker, *Wakefield, its History and People*, 1934.

5. Leisure in Victorian Ossett

by David Scriven

People Mutht Be Amuthed. They can't be alwayth a-learning, nor yet they can't be always a-working, they an't made for it.

SO SAID MR SLEARY, the circus proprietor in Charles Dickens' novel, *Hard Times*. And although in the small industrial town of Ossett hours of work were long and wages were low, people did find the time and the money to enjoy their leisure during Victoria's reign.

Just how much free time they had is difficult to discover because information about working hours in Ossett is limited to a reference in one parliamentary report and rare comments in local newspapers. These show that whereas Spring End Mill worked a seventy-hour week in 1833, by 1905 the usual working week in Ossett's mills had fallen to fifty-six hours. This reflected the situation nationally as under the impact of the *Factory Acts* the working week shortened and Saturday became established as a half holiday.

Evidence about working hours in the town's coal mines is even scarcer than that from the textile industry, but in 1841 the pits belonging to Joshua Smithson worked a ten-hour day while in 1889 it was claimed that one local colliery was working eleven and a half hours a day seven days a week.[1] One small group who certainly worked excessive hours in the late Victorian period were the town's shop assistants: before they gained a half day holiday in 1891 they served for 70 to 80 hours a week.

While hours of work declined, wages increased during the Victorian period. Again information about Ossett is rare, but it does suggest a rise in incomes. Most handloom weavers in the town were earning a maximum of twelve shillings a week in 1853, while by 1905 the maximum weekly wage for male textile workers was twenty-two shillings and for female textile workers it was twelve shillings. However, Ossett had the reputation locally of being a low-wage town. Some 200 Ossett hand-loom weavers were working for masters in Dewsbury, Batley and Batley Carr in 1853 because they paid more than Ossett masters and in 1889 and again in 1905 the *Yorkshire Factory Times* commented on the low wages prevalent in the town's textile trades.[2] Despite this, an increasing amount of money flowed into the local savings banks in the late nineteenth century. At one branch of the Yorkshire Penny Bank, for example, the sum on deposit rose from £2,041 in 1873 to £31, 664 in 1894.

The leisure habits of the people of Ossett showed both continuity and change in the Victorian years. One traditional institution that retained its attraction throughout this period, and that played a central role in the leisure hours of many of the town's men, was the public house. The town's inns and taverns were licensed to sell a range of alcoholic drinks, while the beer-houses could only sell ale. Both types of pub increased in numbers in the town. There were fourteen inns and taverns and seven beer-houses in the town in 1838 and this had risen to twenty-two inns and taverns and thirteen beer-houses in 1901.[3] Of course, the population increased between the two years and it actually rose more quickly than the number of pubs. A snapshot of pub use is given by a census carried out on a Sunday evening in February 1882 by the local Band of Hope Union: 2,197 people, some twenty per cent of the population, entered the thirty-five pubs in the town, including 200 women and 150 children sent out for drink for home consumption. The pubs were not, however, solely places for drinking. Gossip was exchanged, newspapers such as *Bell's* were read and games including quoits, keys and brasses and bowls were played. Pubs also served as the meeting places of various clubs and societies, among them friendly societies like the Oddfellows who in 1838 met at the *Old Hare and Hounds* for their anniversary dinner.

During the late Victorian period the establishment of political and working men's clubs in the town provided additional places for the town's men to socialise. The Conservatives formed their club in 1867 and in 1881 they opened a purpose built clubhouse in New Street. Although the Liberals were stronger than the Conservatives in Ossett, they did not found their club until 1874 and it was not until 1894 that they opened their clubhouse in Station Road (Figure 1). The South Ossett Working Man's Institute, which linked to South Ossett parish church, was created in 1870 and by 1897 there were also working men's clubs on Queen Street and Street Side. These clubs could not, however, rival the popularity of the pubs and club members were often pub users.

Victorian critics of the pubs blamed them for encouraging drunkenness and for wasting the working man's money. One tactic of temperance reformers was to restrict the availability of alcohol by limiting opening hours, while another was to provide alternative venues for working men to socialise. In Ossett the Temperance

Figure 1. The Ossett Liberal Club's building on Station Road, which was the work of W A Kendall, was opened in 1894. *Courtesy Ossett Historical Society.*

Society, founded in 1848, provided what became known as the Saloon, a place where members could read newspapers, play draughts and chess and talk without the presence of drink. The Saloon was never able to rival the public houses in popularity, but this did not prevent Charles Hallgath from launching a commercial temperance venture, a Cocoa House in Dearden Street, in 1879.

Like some other temperance advocates, Hallgath was a vegetarian. In this he showed much more respect for animal life than some other Victorians. The traditional sports of dog and cock fighting were outlawed in 1835, but the difficulty of enforcing the law in an under policed society meant that both activities continued. Two public houses in Ossett, the *Hare and Hounds* and the *Cock and Bottle*, were until at least the 1850s regular venues for cock fights(Figure 2). The opening of a police station in Ossett in the 1860s made it much more difficult to arrange such events, but a taste for sports involving cruelty to animals remained. Rabbit coursing was held weekly at nearby Chickenley in 1884, while two years earlier 200 to 300 people

Figure 2. The *Cock and Bottle* in 2001.

had gathered to watch a local character called 'Wild Jack' worry a hedgehog with his teeth.

There were leisure pursuits involving animals that did not involve bloodshed. Among them was pigeon racing which by the 1890s in Ossett had enough supporters to warrant the formation of three clubs, the Ossett Town Homing Society, the Ossett and District Homing Society and the Ossett Common Homing Society. Some townspeople were prejudiced against pigeon racing. Councillor G H Wilson, President of the Ossett and District Homing Society, admitted that he had believed that it would be a 'disgrace' to be associated with such an organisation, but had since realised that the sport was as 'pure' as any other.[4] From the 1890s the town's annual agricultural show gave the pigeon fanciers, together with the local dog and rabbit breeders, the opportunity to show the public their skills.

The agricultural show also gave gardeners a chance to display their produce to the public. Those who promoted gardening sometimes did so because they believed that it was an alternative to less desirable working class activities. Reporting in 1838 on the first show of the Ossett Horticultural Society, the *Wakefield Journal* commented that workers 'should be encouraged to join so that they devote themselves to the cultivation of flowers and fruit rather than visiting beer houses.' The show was held in the *Cock and Bottle*.[5]

Although some traditional sports such as dog and cock fighting withered in Victoria's reign, others survived. Among them in Ossett was knurr and spell, a sport sometimes known as the poor man's golf. One of the attractions of the game was that it could be played for high stakes. When in 1882 a match took place between an Ossett man and a Bradford man the prize was as much as £50. Much more popular than knurr and spell were two other sports with long histories, cricket and football. Modern cricket was developed in the eighteenth century, but football had to wait until Victoria's reign before the rules of soccer and rugby were codified. These games were valued by some because of their supposedly character forming nature. For B P Wilson of Ossett outdoor games taught the virtues 'of alertness, courage, courtesy and self-control' that were useful in every walk of life.[6]

In Ossett the Mechanics' Institute, founded in 1850, fielded a cricket team that on at least two occasions in the 1860s arranged matches between Parr's All England XI and a XXII from Ossett. Lack of support resulted in the failure of the team in 1873, but in the following year it was restarted as the Perseverance Club, a name that was soon changed to the Ossett Cricket Club. As the town's premier cricket club it won the Heavy Woollen Cup in 1884 (Figure 3). Other

Figure 3. The Ossett cricket team in 1888. Several of its members were long-standing members of the Ossett Club. A F Glover was a playing member of its first team for twenty-seven years during which time he scored 8,144 runs in 385 completed innings.

teams, of course, also existed in late Victorian Ossett, among them teams from Pildacre Mill, South Ossett Working Men's Institute and the Green Congregational Church.

The Rugby Union was formed in 1871 and in 1876 a 'Lover of Sport' wrote to the Ossett Observer urging the formation of a rugby team in the town. He was clearly aware that some people regarded rugby as dangerous, but he tried to reassure his readers by claiming that it was 'no more dangerous than cricket playing' and that any accidents were the result of 'sheer carelessness' or 'want of knowledge of the rules.'[7] A rugby team was formed in connection with the Perseverance Cricket Club in the following year and in 1881 it became an independent organisation. For over twenty years the club was in the Yorkshire Union and was the leading rugby club in the town, but in 1899 it was reformed when it joined the Northern League. Supporters of the change argued that it would improve the club's prospects as it would be able to give greater financial incentives to its players and it would play against better teams. They were wrong: in 1905 the club was dissolved. The local newspaper gave three reasons for the club's failure: a lack of talent, a lack of support and a lack of money. It summed up the situation in the words, 'when footballers are bought and sold like packets of tea or cattle on Wakefield market, the clubs with the longest purses survive.'[8] Although Ossett Rugby Club was the town's leading team, a number of lesser rugby teams also played in the town during the late Victorian period among them Ossett Clarence and Ossett Common.

Although the Football Association was created in 1863, it was not until the last years of Victoria's reign that soccer gained much support in Ossett. The Ossett Association Football Club was formed in 1897, but it proved to be short lived. However, a number of other teams were also formed including South Ossett Albion and Ossett Juniors. Two other late Victorian sports that found followers in Ossett were cycling and lawn tennis. Ossett Bicycle Club was formed in 1882 and its first outing was to Boston Spa. The Ossett club followed the example of other cyclists by adopting a uniform. It was olive brown in colour and was judged as being 'neat and appropriate' by the *Ossett Observer*.[9] The introduction of the safety bicycle in 1886 made cycling more popular, but traditionalists objected to women cyclists. John Wilson, a local cycle agent, tried to reassure potential customers by advertising the Duke of Westminster's statement that he saw 'no objection to women cycling in moderation.'[10] It was perhaps to create publicity for his wares that in 1896 Wilson joined David Ellwood on a ride from Ossett to London, a trip the two completed in twenty-three hours and five minutes. More socially exclusive than cycling was lawn tennis. Like cycling, however, it appealed to women as well as men. Its rules were codified in 1874 and by 1887 Ossett had its own lawn tennis club. This appears to have been short lived, but in 1904 the Ossett Cricket Club felt that there was sufficient interest in tennis to justify laying out three courts for its members.

'Ossett is a musical town' commented the *Wakefield Express* in 1906. This musical tradition went back into Victoria's reign and was nourished by the choral and instrumental music of the local churches and chapels. Like other Yorkshire towns Ossett supported a choral society. Formed possibly in 1837, its repertoire was dominated by sacred music. Handel's *Messiah* and *Judas Maccabaeus*, Haydn's *Creation*, and Mendelssohn's *Elijah* were all performed by the society. On occasions principals were hired to supplement the local singers. For the 1868 performance of *Judas Maccabaeus*, for example, principals were engaged from Leeds, Manchester and Oldham. Apart from the choral society, Ossett was also able to support a glee and madrigal society in the 1850s. This had lapsed by the 1890s, but in 1900 the Ossett Borough Glee and Madrigal Society was formed.

Ossett was also able to support a number of brass bands in the Victorian period. Two bands existed in the town by the 1850s, the Ossett and the Gawthorpe bands, but the impact of the temperance movement apparently caused both to split into temperance and non-temperance bands. In the 1870s the division was healed by the foundation of the Gawthorpe Victoria Brass Band and the Ossett United Brass and Reed Band. The latter became the Ossett Borough

Figure 4. The Station Road premises of the Mechanics' Institute and Technical School were opened in 1890 and were built to the design of an Ossett architect, W A Kendall. *Ossett Historical Society.*

Brass Band when the town gained a charter in 1890. Finance was often a problem for brass bands as rooms needed to be hired for practices and instruments had to be bought. When the Gawthorpe Victoria Band was formed four of its members had to lend the band £10 each so that the fifteen instruments needed could be bought from their Manchester makers. It was presumably to raise funds that at Christmas the Ossett Band toured the town visiting its friends from at least the 1880s.

Self-improvement was a theme stressed by Victorian moralists and Ossett did not lack its share of self-improvers. The Mechanics' Institute was founded in 1850 and it provided its members with a reading room, lectures and evening classes. Like so many other recreational activities in the Victorian period, however, it was dominated by men (Figure 4). Churches and chapels also encouraged self-improvement by creating mutual improvement societies. One of the most active belonged to the Green Congregational Church during the ministry of J P Perkins in the 1870s and the 1880s. It was not afraid to debate contentious political issues such as the rights and wrongs of the Afghan war.

Essential to self-improvement were books, but not all books were good books according to Victorian self improvers. Dr Neary, vicar of South Ossett, warned the committee of the Mechanics' Institute in 1855 that 'many a brilliant mind had been poisoned by some of the cheap publications.'[11] However, the Mechanics' Institute provided its members with a library that by 1890 had over 1,000 volumes. In addition, in the same year, the town had six circulating libraries including one belonging to the Cockburns, the stationers and publishers of the *Ossett Observer*. The one guinea subscription to the Cockburns' library gave readers access to a collection of 700 volumes that was replenished from Mudie's Select London Library.

Access to the library of the Mechanics' Institute and to the circulating libraries was restricted to those who could afford their subscriptions, but an *Act of Parliament* of 1850 permitted towns to found free public libraries financed from the rates. When, however, a meeting took place at Ossett Grammar School in 1890 to consider the adoption of the Act, a majority of the thirty gentlemen present felt that the move was premature. Seven years later public opinion was more favourable and Ossett Borough Council celebrated Queen Victoria's Diamond Jubilee by taking responsibility for library of the Mechanics' Institute. Ossett's readers appreciated their new public library mainly for the fiction that it provided: in 1899-1900 eighty-eight per cent of the issues were novels. Some councillors were highly critical of this development, but Alderman Cox took a more tolerant view:

> *There were novels and novels and some were not only interesting, but edifying... and he did not mind books being published which would create an occasional outburst of laughter.*[12]

Victorian reformers were sometimes critical of traditional feasts because they promoted drunkenness, immorality and disorder. As a result some towns lost their feasts, but in Ossett the Feast increased in popularity in the Victorian period. Originally held to celebrate the feast of the Holy Trinity in June, the Ossett Feast still had religious associations because a number of the town's Sunday schools held their annual walks during Feast week. The processions of children visited the homes of their schools' patrons, sang hymns and finished the day with tea and games. Another feature of the Feast was drinking in the town's pubs, but this appears to have become more restrained in Victoria's reign. The *Ossett Observer* remarked in 1867 that whereas 'violence, drunkenness and outrage' had once marked the Feast, it had become almost 'harmless and innocent.'[13] A third feature of the Feast was the fair. By 1861 there were sixty-five stalls and attractions included spice and nut stalls, penny peep shows, shooting galleries, photographic artists, cheap Jacks, swing boats and steam horses. Finally, the Feast was accompanied by galas with music and dancing and by cricket matches. To the Feast came not only the people of Ossett, but also visitors from Wakefield, Dewsbury and Horbury and the opening of the local railway in the 1860s made it much easier for them to get to the Feast.

For some businessmen the timing of the Feast was an inconvenience: while Ossett feasted other towns worked and while

Ossett worked other towns feasted. In 1880, after unsuccessful previous attempts, a public meeting agreed to the move the Feast from June to the August Bank Holiday. However, not all of the townspeople agreed with the alteration and the Old Feast continued to be celebrated. To make their point some of them marked the 1881 Feast by parading through Dale Street a hearse painted with a skull and cross bones and bearing placards with the announcement, 'Interment of the New Feast.'[14]

Apart from Ossett Feast itself, which occurred in the town centre, there were a number of smaller-scale feasts held in other parts of the town from time to time during Victoria's reign. Perhaps the most interesting was Gawthorpe Maypole Festival. In the 1840s a maypole was still erected in Ossett. Whether this was a revival or a survival of an old festival is unknown, but certainly in 1850 a new maypole was put up in the middle of Gawthorpe. Unfortunately, the pole was soon felled by a combination of vandalism and high wind. However, in 1875 a new red, white and blue maypole topped by a weathercock was raised and the Maypole Festival was resurrected. Among its features were a fair and the May Queen's procession, although in 1877 a straw filled figure took the place of the Queen.

Commercial pleasure grounds were a characteristic of the leisure industry in the Georgian and Victorian periods. Matthew Wharton, a Batley businessman, believed that Ossett Spa was ripe for development as such a ground. At Easter in 1884 he opened the Montpellier Pleasure Grounds there. Although the music, acrobats, comedians and a high wire artist, the African Blondin, attracted a good attendance, the venture bankrupted Wharton. It was then revealed that he had a history of financial failures in the textile and entertainment industries, including the loss of £1,000 leasing a pier on the Isle of Man. The Montpellier Pleasure Grounds did not reopen.

Ossett attracted professional entertainers not only during the town's feasts, but at other times as well. From at least 1863 circuses including Sanger's, Pinder's and Fossett's found it worthwhile to visit the town. Not all of them lived up to the people's expectations. The grand procession of Hayes' Circus in 1871 was described by the *Ossett Observer* as a 'sorry affair' that provoked 'much laughter.'[15] Travelling theatre companies also played in the town from at least 1864. The proprietors of these companies were clearly aware that in some circles the morality of their offerings was regarded with deep suspicion. Thus in 1879 Vickers' Royal Alhambra Theatre reassured the public that 'a visit could be paid without causing a blush to mantle the cheek of the most fastidious.'[16]. It was usual for each company to perform several plays during its stay in the town. During the week that Newell's Pavilion Theatre was in Ossett in 1884 it performed six dramas ranging from *Othello* to a temperance play called *Father Come Home* or *Ten Nights in a Bar Room*. At the 1898 Old Feast a new form of entertainment reached Ossett: the moving picture. An enterprising showman put on a film show featuring the bombardment of Manila during the Spanish-American War. A few years later the townspeople were able to watch the funeral of Queen Victoria on film.

During Victoria's long reign there were some significant changes in leisure in Ossett. The more barbaric traditional leisure activities, cock and dog fighting, were driven underground, while new forms of recreation such as soccer, rugby and cycling developed. The dominance of the public house as a place for socialising was challenged by the emergence of political and working men's clubs. Rational recreation was promoted by the Mechanics' Institute and by the mutual improvement societies. Yet there were also strong elements of continuity. In particular, the public house remained central to the leisure activities of many working class men. As a result of this combination of change and continuity there were, by 1901, a greater variety of leisure activities open to Ossett's people than there had been in 1837.

Notes and References

This essay is based mainly on three newspapers, the *Wakefield Journal and West Riding Herald*, the *Wakefield Express* and the *Ossett Observer*. The national background to the developments sketched here is outlined in chapter five of Edward Royle's, *Modern Britain: A Social History 1750-1997*, (2nd edition, 1997).

1. 'Supplementary Report of the Central Board of Factory Commissioners, Part II, Answers to Queries, North Eastern District ', British Parliamentary Papers, 1834, volume XX, p 280-281; *Yorkshire Factory Times*, 2 August 1889.
2. *Yorkshire Factory Times*, 2. August 1889; 6 January 1905.
3. W White, *Directory of the West Riding of Yorkshire*, volume II, p 390.
4. *Ossett Observer*, 2 November 1901.
5. *Wakefield Journal*, 12 October 1838.
6. *Ossett Observer*, 18 November 1905.
7. *Ossett Observer*, 2 December 1876.
8. *Ossett Observer*, 9 September 1905.
9. *Ossett Observer*, 3 June 1882.
10. *Ossett Observer*, 28 March 1896.
11. *Wakefield Journal*, 5 January 1855.
12. *Ossett Observer*, 1 June 1901.
13. *Ossett Observer*, 22 June 1867.
14. *Ossett Observer*, 8 June 1881.
15. *Ossett Observer*, 15 July 1871.
16. *Ossett Observer*, 21 June 1879.

6. THE STORY OF COOPER BROS (WAKEFIELD) LTD, INCLUDING THE BUS SERVICE OPERATED BY THE FIRM

by J D Clayton

THIS IS THE STORY OF A SMALL FAMILY CONCERN which, from the late 1920s to the mid 1950s, operated a service carrying miners and other employees to one of the collieries on the outskirts of Wakefield. The service ran only at shift times and officially did not carry members of the general public as its route lay within the operating area of the West Riding Automobile Company Ltd and J Bullock and Sons Motor B & S Service, the two main bus companies in the town, and they had the monopoly.

The Cooper family at the beginning lived at 11 Field Lane in what was known as the village of Thornes but which was in effect a suburb of Wakefield. For most of his life Mr Cooper senior was employed at what was then Hodgson and Simpson's soap works, later to become the Spencer Wire Works which was just a few yards down the road from his home. Mrs Cooper originated from Luddenden Foot near Halifax and came to Wakefield when she married Mr Cooper.

The Coopers had four sons, William, Harry, Joe and Fred. There had also been a daughter, Blanche, but she had died in childhood. William had a son, Albert. Harry had a daughter, Mary. Joe had two sons, Harry and Ronald, and Fred had two daughters, Blanche and Annie, and a son, Walter, who was the youngest of the family. On attaining manhood William joined a firm of Bradford dyers. Joe became a carpenter and I am told by a correspondent that he resided in Thornes Road. Harry, who was asthmatic, would appear to have been in the coach business from the very beginning, becoming company secretary, a position he held for many years.

When the business first started it was at premises in Field Lane adjoining an orchard kept by some people named Jessop. The first vehicle owned was a horse and cart which, so far as can be ascertained, was driven by Harry. The business, which commenced about the time of the First World War, consisted of the sale of greengrocery and fruit, the latter probably being obtained from Jessop's orchard. Then somewhere around 1921 the horse and cart was exchanged for a Ford Model T lorry. I think it must have been about then that Fred joined with Harry to do the driving because, as far as I can ascertain and from my own recollection, when the bus service started, Fred did all the driving and Harry acted as conductor.

The firm now became known as Cooper Bros and traded as haulage contractors and charabanc operators. A further venture at this time was the commencement of a coal business and my correspondent again remembers her family buying coal from them, and tells how during the days of the general strike, the brothers would let them have the odd bag or two when they were able to get it. It would most probably also be during this period when Coopers were running the coal business and travelling to and from the pit that they realised the need of those miners who lived some distance away for some means of transport between their homes and work at the beginning and end of each shift. This need resulted in the adaptation of the Model T so that it could be fitted with a charabanc body. And so began the bus service. The charabanc lorry could also be hired out at weekends and other convenient times, when not required for carrying miners to and from work, for trips and excursions, and this, in fact was done, hence the adoption by the firm of the title already mentioned.

In 1929 or thereabouts the Model T Ford was replaced by two normal buses. This meant that the firm needed commodious premises and a move was made to a yard at the junction of Ings Road and Denby Dale Road, now part of Sainsbury's supermarket. The yard was owned by a man named Charles, or Charlie, Laycock, who was a tinsmith and lived at 113 Thornes Road. The new garage, if my memory serves me correctly, was sited in the middle of the yard with its entrance opposite the gateway into Denby Dale Road, thus giving easy access for the buses entering or leaving. It was at this time that the firm was put on a proper business footing and became a limited company taking the title Cooper Bros (Wakefield) Ltd.

The two buses which were the cause of this move were a Thorneycroft and a Leyland PLSC Lion. I remember these two buses quite well, the Thorneycroft better than the Lion although I was a boy of only about seven or eight years old. At that time I was attending St James Church of England Junior School in Thornes Lane and came back home at dinner time. One of the routes I used to take back to school after dinner was from Thornes Road into Major Street then along Major Street across what I believe was called the Piece into Field Lane and then into Thornes Lane (Figure 1). By so doing I cut off a very large corner and saved myself quite a considerable walk. Anybody knowing the Thornes area will be

Figure 1. Major Street, Thornes, still with bollards separating it from Field Lane.

familiar with this road. In passing I should say that Major Street was a cul-de-sac with a barrier at the far end, at that time consisting of posts and a chain so that pedestrian traffic and cyclists could get through but not vehicles. For the greater part of his life Fred lived at 20 Major Street and when he had finished the morning shift he would bring his bus across the Piece, park it at the chain and post barrier and walk the few yards down Major Street to his house until it was time to go out again for the afternoon shift. Usually the bus was the Thorneycroft although occasionally the Lion did appear.

Even at that tender age I was very interested in buses and came to know the Thorneycroft quite well. The bus was painted blue and was a very handsome vehicle. It was what was most likely known as an 'A' type, a type which was produced in the mid to late twenties and was a normal-control vehicle, that was one which had the engine out front and the driver inside with the passengers. The seating capacity was for twenty passengers on what were for the period quite comfortable seats. Whether or not this and the Lion were purchased new I do not know. Likewise unfortunately I do not know the body manufacturer nor its registration number.

The Lion was what was termed a Long Lion. This type could seat up to thirty-five passengers as opposed to the shorter version which could seat thirty-one. This bus had rear-entrance bodywork, again, I regret to say, of unknown manufacture, and was of the half cab variety, that is with the driver sitting alongside the engine. The exact seating capacity again is not known. The seating was quite luxurious and was covered in either rexine or leather. Later on in its life, if I remember correctly, the seats were recovered in moquette. I well recollect seeing this bus in use on the colliery service with Harry conducting and Fred driving. This particular bus was also used for private hire and one rather interesting and unusual occasion when it was so used comes to my mind. Most Wakefield people, I am sure, if they don't remember the Wakefield Pageant which took place in Clarence Park in 1933, will at least have heard of it (Figure 2). Considerable numbers of people came from round about by coach to see the show and Thornes Road, which had nothing like the amount of traffic on it that it has now, was used as a coach park. On one evening a coach broke down just as it was about to set off on its return journey and was not capable of quick repair. As a result a relief coach had to be found to get the party home and the one used was Coopers' Lion.

With the passing of the *Road Traffic Acts* of 1930 and 1933, as well as various regulations controlling services, restrictions also came into force regulating the size of vehicles allowed on the roads, and, to Fred's disgust, the Lion was adjudged to be one and a half inches too wide and was therefore prohibited from use. I do not know the exact date when it was taken off the road but I have been told that it eventually became a showman's vehicle, again much to Fred's disgust as he felt that, if it could be used for that purpose, then it could be used for his colliery service when it would be carrying out a much more useful function.

Following the withdrawal of the PLSC Lion, it became necessary to obtain a replacement. In 1929 Yorkshire Woollen District Transport of Saville Town, Dewsbury, purchased a batch of Leyland Lion LTI buses with Brush thirty-seat bodies. During the period 1935-37 withdrawal of these buses started to take place and one of them was purchased by Cooper Bros. Unfortunately, although I have searched through PSV Circle and Omnibus Society records giving details of all

Figure 2. The cover for the souvenir brochure for the 1933 Wakefield pageant.

Figure 3. A bus from the Yorkshire Woollen District Transport Co fleet, similar to one acquired by Coopers.

these buses and their ultimate disposal, I can find no record of which one Coopers bought. The undisputed fact remains, however, that one of these buses, with a registration number somewhere between HD 3753 and HD 3769 came into Cooper Bros' possession and was operated by them in Yorkshire Woollen District red, remaining in that colour until its withdrawal during the war (Figure 3). Also about this time I understand Coopers owned a short-wheelbase lorry although for what purpose they used it I am not aware, nor can I recall ever seeing it on the road; possibly they may have continued the coal business or done a little general haulage.

To return to the ex-Yorkshire bus, however, I was now about ten years old and my interest in buses had become much more developed, as a result of which I became really familiar with this bus, particularly as I knew its origins and what its duties were to be. I was therefore able to follow its activities with great interest during the quite considerable period it spent with Coopers. It speaks a lot for the workmanship that went into the construction of these early Leyland buses: this one in particular had spent six or seven years coping with the steep hills that are a feature of the Dewsbury area, and then it spent a further seven or eight years carrying miners to and from Walton Colliery, again no easy task when you consider that it was built to carry thirty passengers and quite frequently it carried more than double that number.

I think that of all the buses that Cooper Bros possessed over the years, the red ex-Yorkshire Woollen District Leyland Lion was the most well-known around Thornes. I know it was so far as I was concerned, and many amusing stories have been told about it, some of which have been passed on to me while gathering material for this account. Apart from the one occasion I have already mentioned of seeing the PLSC Lion in service crewed by Fred and Harry, I have no recollection of seeing it at any other time, nor do I ever remember seeing the Thorneycroft actually carrying passengers, the reason for this no doubt being because I was too young to be allowed into town on my own.

With the red Lion, however, it was a different story. I remember first seeing it in the garage in Laycock's yard on Denby Dale Road when it must have been newly acquired and was in all probability in the process of being made ready for service. By this time I had a bicycle and had also become a pupil at Wakefield Grammar School so that my trips into Wakefield and its environs were frequent, with the result that I became quite familiar with the red bus, particularly when it was on its afternoon duties. These were, of course, only part of those carried out by the vehicle which had to work very hard during its long life as also had Harry and Fred, its faithful crew.

As further vehicles were purchased during the years, two additional drivers, Arthur and Sydney Bell, were employed.

The first trip was about six o'clock in the morning to get the 'early turn' to work. Fred and Harry would arrive at the garage to collect the bus at about 5.30am having walked there from their homes whatever the weather. The brothers would then have to get the bus started, most likely by cranking as I do not imagine it would be fitted with such a thing as a self-starter; this would be no easy task at the best of times, still less on a cold winter's morning when there was a degree or two of frost on the ground or an inch or two of snow, but Coopers had a reputation for getting their customers to work and the weather had to be very bad for them to fail to get through. The bus was then driven to Thornes Lane where its first stop was the LMS railway bridge opposite the house of Arthur Bell, the joiner and undertaker (Figure 4). Another of my correspondents, who lived a few doors away from Mr Bell, told me that the bus made an excellent alarm clock because when it came to set off again, not having time to get really warmed up, it tended to backfire on all cylinders, thus effectively waking him up and probably half the neighbourhood as well; at any rate he said that while the bus was running he was never late for school.

From this point the Lion proceeded on its way along Thornes Lane to Kirkgate picking up passengers at various points on the way, thence along Kirkgate to the Springs which was its main pick-up point, by which time it was just about half full. When those waiting at the Springs had climbed aboard, Fred had a fairish load, with the result that with any further passengers picked up *en route*, by the time

Figure 4. The L M S railway bridge crossing Thornes Lane which was Coopers' first pick-up point on the colliery run. Field Lane is on the left.

he reached the collliery the bus was pretty well packed to the doors – and Fred had never been known to leave anybody behind, in fact he had been heard to say that on occasions he had carried as many as seventy passengers. Even with ten standing it would be quite a tight squeeze, but with an extra forty – well, I just don't know how he got them on, especially when one considers that miners were not particularly small people. However confirmation that he did get them on comes from one of my correspondents who recalls that on one occasion when Fred was pulled up by the police for overloading, they counted seventy-six men which led to the policeman asking whether, as they got out at the front, they were going round the back and getting in again at the emergency door.

The majority of miners were very much addicted to smoking pipes, which contained usually either shag or twist tobacco, both of which have an exceedingly pungent, not to say obnoxious, smell. So if you get a bus with forty or more miners aboard most of whom are smoking shag or twist it can well be imagined that the atmosphere could be just about cut with a knife. Harry, Fred's conductor, was asthmatic and I remember Cyril Hudson, the local Thornes barber, telling me on one occasion when I had called in to get my hair cut and the conversation had somehow got round to Fred and Harry, that poor Harry suffered very acutely when he was on the coach, particularly on the early shift.

The next run was timed for mid morning and it was then when I used to see the Lion when I was cycling in the Thornes and Kirkgate area of Wakefield. The same route was followed as that taken for the early shift but the one thing that always fascinated me was the order Fred used to pick up his passengers. In Kirkgate he picked up at the normal bus stops but on the inward journey, on his way to the Springs, whereas I would have thought it more logical to proceed to the Springs, pick up the passengers waiting there, and then pick up in Kirkgate as he drove towards Walton, in the same manner as ordinary service buses, but no doubt Fred had his reasons.

In the afternoon the runs were reversed, the bus being occupied in bringing the miners back into town at the end of their shift, the only difference being that it did not go into Thornes and those going to that area had to disembark at the bottom of Kirkgate. There were also evening runs, presumably taking the men who were on night shift to work and possibly bringing the afternoon shift home. I am told that Fred and Harry would arrive home somewhere round about 10 o'clock. Whether or not they had called at the local pub for refreshment I do not know but the fact remains that they had done a good day's work by the time they finished.

Cooper Bros' involvement with the transport of miners to and from work at Walton Colliery went on into the post-war years. As the thirties progressed, however, bus and coach operators became more and more concerned with another side of the business - day trips and private hire work (Figure 5). In the early part of the decade Coopers had not engaged very much in this type of work but as the thirties drew to a close the firm began to take greater interest in it. With this activity in mind, and because of the need for an additional bus for the Walton service, the firm purchased from Lansdowne Coachways of Blackpool an almost new Bedford coach which I believe had the designation OB and which had a twenty-six seat forward-entrance body by Plaxton's of Scarborough. Lansdowne Coachways was still in existence recently and operated from premises in Morecambe.

I well remember this coach and in fact had a couple of trips in it. One was a Town Hall NALGO trip to a pantomime in Leeds in the early years of the war when it was driven by Arthur Bell. The other trip was after the war and was another NALGO one to a town, I

Figure 5. An outing from the Queen's Head, now the Queen's Arms, in Denby Dale Road, with the two Leyland Comets and their drivers.

believe, in South Yorkshire for a tennis match. In order to protect the seats on this coach when transporting miners, Cooper had a set of loose covers made.

With the outbreak of war in 1939 great changes took place in the bus and coach industry. Petrol was very scarce and coach trips were at a minimum except for short ones such as visits to the pantomime. The miners' service still continued of course because coal mining was now an essential industry and the old red Lion still continued to give sterling service.

I had now left school and was employed in the Town Hall until 1943 when I was called up for military service so for a number of years I saw very little of Coopers' buses. I did note, however, on the occasions when I came home on leave that the Lion had finally been retired, or perhaps had retired itself as by this time it was getting very decrepit both engine-wise and very definitely as regards body-work. One of the former regular travellers said to me,

> *You had to be very careful where you put your hands when you were on it otherwise you could find yourself getting your fingers trapped by the movement of the body-work and it was not unknown for you to see the road as you were going along.*

Before drawing the final curtain on the Lion I should just like to retell another story regarding this veteran. Living as they did in Thornes and being well-known in the village, Coopers' buses were often used on such occasions as Sunday School outings, particularly from Christ Church situated at the lower end of Thornes Lane near the river which, in the 1930s and early 40s had a very thriving Sunday School, but which is now sadly demolished. The Sunday School outing usually consisted of a trip to a local farmer's field where there was fun and games and tea. I particularly remember one of these outings involving the Lion, although I did not actually take part in it. On this occasion it was to a field somewhere in the Horbury or Middlestown area and to get there the bus had to pass my house on Thornes Road, and I went out to wave to them. Now one of the helpers at this party was my next-door neighbour, Mrs Annie Shaw who, with her husband John Shaw, was a very active member of Christ Church. It had been arranged that, as the bus was passing her house, it would pick Mrs Shaw up on the way, but, such was the number of teachers and children travelling, there was no room for Mr Shaw and he had to arrange alternative transport. When the bus arrived, I was amazed to see the vicar hanging onto the bottom step and the inside a packed mass of humanity. Mrs Shaw was squeezed aboard, the vicar clambered back on and off the bus went. For the children, no doubt, a trip like that added to the excitement of the outing. On finishing the journey, Fred came back to continue his normal duties returning on the completion of festivities to bring the Sunday School home.

I never discovered what happened to the old Lion after withdrawal. I expect it ended up in a scrapyard.

Following the departure of the Lion, a brand-new bus was purchased. This was another Bedford, the wartime version of the popular pre-war OB, only this time it was designated OWB, the W standing for wartime. These OWBs were the only single-decker buses allowed by the Ministry of War Transport, and although built by several body-builders such as, for example, Chas H Roe and Duple, they were all to one standard design, what was termed during wartime as utility. They were only allowed one opening window on each side and had rather cramped seating for thirty-two passengers, the earliest ones being of the wooden slatted variety which I should imagine was quite an advantage when the majority of passengers were miners in their dirty pit clothes. Later types, however, were provided with upholstered seats. Coopers were fortunate in being allocated two of these buses, the second having upholstery. I have no doubt that the reason for a small firm like Coopers being allowed two buses was because coal mining was an essential industry and the miners had to be got to work. As far as I can remember the wooden seated OWB was numbered AHL92, the one with upholstered seats was also in the AHL series but I cannot bring the number to mind.

After the war a relaxation in travel took place and, although petrol was still rationed and cars were scarce, a few new buses were beginning to come through although by no means enough to satisfy requirements. In addition the services of coach operators were beginning to be in great demand as people were eager to have a change of scenery after the restrictions of wartime, with trips to the countryside and coast. As a result, considerable numbers of coaches which had been laid up during the war years were brought out of mothballs and many and varied types of vehicles of a variety of ages began to appear on English roads.

At this time, apart from the two OWBs used on the colliery service, Cooper Bros had only the twenty-six seater Bedford coach purchased in 1938 but, realising that trips were becoming popular, the management decided it was time to expand. They already had some experience of private-hire work with the convertible lorry/charabanc, the Long Lion and the Bedford, but the time had

Figure 6. The Mark II Leyland Comets.

come to branch out into bigger things. In the immediate post-war years, therefore, two luxury coaches were purchased. These were very unusual vehicles in that they were Mark II Leyland Comets. The Leyland Comet was normally a goods vehicle but a very few were given coach bodies and, to the best of my knowledge, these were the only two in the Wakefield area. I cannot recall ever seeing any others in my journeys around the countryside. The vehicles had Plaxton coach bodies and were registered CHL 582, purchased in 1949, and DHL 130, purchased in 1950. For a considerable period they were driven by Arthur (DHL 130) and Sydney (CHL 582) Bell (Figures 6 and 7). I never remember travelling on the CHL coach but I had several trips on the DHL when it was hired for choir outings by Christ Church, and very comfortable they were too.

Shortly after this a further Leyland Comet was acquired second-hand from Ellen Smith Tours of Wigan which had an Arlington body, a make with which, I regret to say, I am not familiar. I did, however, have a ride on it on the occasion of the choir trip to Morecambe. This coach was classed as a touring coach and had very comfortable seats upholstered in red hide, but it had one rather odd seat at the front: this was a very small seat for one, by the entrance, with its back in a corner formed by the windscreen and the door and facing diagonally across the coach. I would imagine that in its days as a touring vehicle, this would have been the seat used by the courier. It was not particularly popular

Figure 7. Peter Wilkinson pictured with one of the Coopers' Leyland Comets. He recalls Coopers' buses being engaged for trips with Thornes Youth Club.

Figure 8. Coopers' garage premises in Thornes Road with a number of their coaches.

with the passengers and when we travelled on it the younger members usually took turns to sit on it.

The next coach to arrive was also second-hand and was a Maudslay which came via Comberhill Motors of Ings Road, a well-known Wakefield motor-dealer in its day but now long closed. This coach was also bodied by Plaxton and was a very comfortable vehicle. I was fortunate in being able to have a ride on it with Arthur Bell as driver, this time as an invited guest with the Mothers' Union. Further Bedford coaches were purchased during this period. These were twenty-nine seater vehicles with Duple bodywork, obtained from Charles Wensley of Ings Road and Comberhill Motors, but as I was working away at this time and only at home in the evening and at weekends, I never became familiar with them.

In 1956 the firm ceased business. In the years since the First World War the company had grown from a small coal and greengrocery business coupled with a local colliery bus service to one of the major coach-hire firms in the area, and its blue and cream coaches were a familiar sight in the district. Up to a short time ago its garage in the yard of the former Lyons' bakery on Thornes Road was still in existence but it has recently been demolished so all trace of Cooper Bros (Wakefield) Ltd has now disappeared except for the memories (Figure 8).

Acknowledgments

My thanks to Mr Walter Cooper for the information he has so kindly given me concerning Cooper Bros (Wakefield) Ltd. My thanks also for his kind offer to read and check the finished history. Many thanks also to those who took the trouble to write of telephone me with information, and also those who gave or loaned me photographs; without their help and that of Mr Cooper this history would not have been written.

7. The Zivilinternierunglasger at Lofthouse Park

by Peter Wood

THE SIXTY-ACRE ENTERTAINMENT PARK which had been created by the Yorkshire (West Riding) Electric Tramway Co Ltd at Lofthouse was, to the War Government of 1914, suitable for the internment of aliens and as a POW camp. The park was on a tramway route, between towns, in the countryside and in a fairly isolated position. It was taken over and made ready to hold the large number of German, Austrians and Turks[1] that were living, working or holidaying in England when hostilities broke out.

Until recently, there has been no information regarding Lofthouse Internment Camp. In 1997 a German lawyer[2] studying for his doctorate found the papers, in Germany, of one of the internees and sent copies to an English acquaintance in the Anglo-German Society. The lawyer thought that the study would be of interest to the Society and asked them for information about Lofthouse Park where his study subject was interned.

Hermann J Held (1890-1963) in the early summer of 1914 was studying for a law degree in Freiburg and to complete his studies required some literature from the Squire Library at Cambridge and the British Museum Foreign Office Library in London. Through one of his tutors, Dr. Otto Keollreutter, he was put in contact with a Professor Dr Lassa Oppenheim already teaching at Cambridge on International Law. The arrangement when finalised was that Held would holiday, then visit Oppenheim and possibly, as there were an number of important lectures he wished to hear, stay in England during the Autumn to attend them.

Held was not a stranger to Cambridge for he had been there in 1912, where he had been noticed attending a large political rally. This visit had been noted by Special Branch and would be appraised if any conflict occurred. His interest at that time was in 'English behaviour of Naval warfare' and he was more concerned about economics and legalities than enquiries about the strengths of the Fleet.

The term had not started when on 3 August war was declared and Held, along with many other students and lecturers, was now unable to return to Germany. There were special permits allowing aliens to return within a specific time but either Held did not know of them or else he was too busy with his studies.

However, *The Aliens Restrictions Order* of August 1914 for Germans in Great Britain prevented his departure and he was arrested, possibly on suspicion of his 'political activities' in 1912, or as a potential spy, but shortly afterwards he was released under police supervision and was allowed to continue his studies. His 'freedom' ended when he was interned on the 21 October with others to Zivilinterierungslager Lofthouse Park. The title indicates that at this moment Lofthouse was an internment camp for civilians, not people in uniform. The internees were not issued with any prison clothing or any clothing which marked them as aliens. Held would remain in England throughout the war, although by April 1918 he would be transferred to the camp at Knockaloe on the Isle of Man (Figure 1).

The camp at Lofthouse consisted of three compounds South, West and North with a total, at that time, of about 1,500 internees, although later on in the war, uniformed Prisoners of War would be sent to the camp pushing the numbers to over 2,400 before many of the internees were moved on and Lofthouse became a Prisoner of War Camp for Armed Forces.

The majority of the camp personnel were people who had a business interest in England, and for one reason or another had not taken out naturalisation papers. In Wakefield at this time there were several German pork butchers and in at least one family the child born in England, carried on the trade while the father, still a German was treated as alien and became interned.

The camp at Lofthouse had been an entertainment park for the West Riding Tramway Company so there were dining rooms, lavatories and the necessary services already installed. The park had been fenced around to keep the non-paying public out and now was

Figure 1. A letter addressed to Hermann Held at Lofthouse Park in 1916.

Figure 2. Some of the internees at Lofthouse Park 1915-1918. Dr Held is the third man from the right, with his hands in his pockets.

used to keep the internees in. The 'rape of Belgium', later the sinking of the Lusitania[3] and the loss of many local young men in the armed forces made something of a role reversal for the fence by keeping the angered public from the internees.

To pass time for the young and physically active there were games to be played, for the Lofthouse Park had six tennis courts, football pitches, a bowling green, an athletic arena, gymnasium and a lake. Some internees turned to gardening for relaxation and to help with their own finances. There was also a theatrical group which produced plays and when they were transferred to Knockaloe they were able to tour that camp with two of their plays. But time must have gone by slowly for most of the internees.

Many of Held's fellows were students and intellectuals of one profession or another who needed mental stimulation and exercise to break the boredom of this enforced captivity. They may have hoped to use their captivity usefully to increase their knowledge and academic advancement.

Held would not have been the only person in the camp who was unprepared for this enforced stay. There must have been many Germans who in the Spring and Summer of 1914 had made the trip to England and Held would have had little with him but a suitcase with clothing and essentials for the relatively short period he intended to stay. He would have brought only enough money for his anticipated stay and certainly he would have to find some way of to eke out his meagre financial means. The only photograph of Held is of a smartly dressed gentleman in company with other similarly dressed men and several dogs. standing outside a wooden hut

(Figure 2). One must assume that he and other men (there is no record of women and children at the camp) must have had the opportunities to have clothing brought to the camp by gentlemen's outfitters from Lofthouse, Leeds or Wakefield.

Fortunately, Held at twenty-four years old had reached an advanced stage in his education, and so he was able to turn to teaching to provide himself with some financial support. It is very possible that he was able to borrow money from the Red Cross or from the richer internees who had businesses on the outside, and still bringing revenue. Whichever course Held took, it was many years after his release that he was able to rid himself of the debt. It must be remembered that Held would have been borrowing in pounds and on his return to Germany he would then be dealing in marks that were rapidly devaluing[4] to valueless.

The records of Hermann Held show that for one of his courses starting on 9 October 1915 there were fifty-seven students, for another course he had sixty students but only seven for a third course. He was in the South Lager in Hut No. 58 and until the authorities recognised these lectures only internees, in the same lager or hut as Held, would have been able to attend any evening meetings.

These *ad hoc* talks that had been organised amongst the prisoners were put on a more official footing when it was decided that from the Summer of 1917 an institutionalised Camp College - University, Vorlesungsv'erzeichnis Lofthouse Park would be established in such a manner that the coursework would be recognised in Germany after the war.[5]

In the camp there were sixty-seven lecturers, some indeed were professors, but all had lectured either in England or Germany and along with the elected Principal, History Professor Dr Herman Waetjen from Freiburg, they felt that they could operate a College of Law to high standards. The military authorities do not seem to have either obstructed or helped with the setting up of the college, save for allowing the 'college authorities' access to material that could only be obtained from outside the camp.

Each compound would hold some courses during the day but each compound was surrounded by a barbed wire fence and with guarded gates leading into them. These gates between compounds must have been closed shortly after 4.45pm. for all the proposed college courses had to be finished by that time, but there were no restrictions in the evenings to lectures attended by inmates of the compound where the lecture was taking place.

In the South Lager the YMCA hall was used, in the West Lager, rooms A. and B. of another YMCA building were in use, while in the North Lager, where the safe was kept, the internees had the use of the big hall (Grosse Halle) and two rooms, A and B in hut 14. These rooms, were partitioned off by a corridor from the medical room and a section of the South YMCA, and an office was created out of the hut 14's luggage room. The double walls of these partitions, made of timber costing £50, were packed with bought sawdust to act as a sound insulation. Cupboards and benches were made by the internees, though stove pipes, linoleum and paint had to be purchased.

Equipment purchased for the administration office, in which would be employed four draughtsmen and two administrative staff, all getting 10 shillings (50p) a week, included typewriter ribbons, duplicating ink, paper and wax sheets, plus all the usual office stationery. To get the college functioning quickly and smoothly it was found necessary to have some material printed outside the camp; these were the passes, leaflets and tickets for attending courses (Figure 3).

Four blackboards, a duplicating machine, a reflex camera and accessories were purchased. The camera photographed 488 sheets of work, possibly to prove the students' and lecturers' abilities once they were back in Germany. Wall charts of the Earth, Africa, North and South America, but not of Europe, (so did the military authorities regard this map as possible escape material?), were bought. Chemicals and equipment for experimentation and scientific

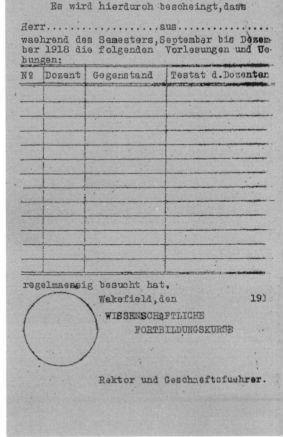

(Mr...from...has during the term Sept - Dec 1918 attended the following lectures and workshops.....Signed.....director and business leader.)

Figure 3. A form for recording attendance at classes at Lofthouse Park.

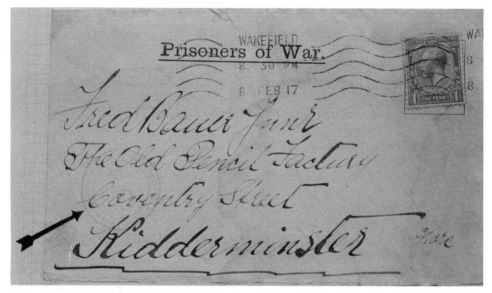

Figure 4. A letter - perhaps with an order for pencils or with payment - to the pencil factory at Kidderminster.

observation, mathematical drawing equipment, artists' paints, crayons, pastels, erasers, pencils, drawing pins and different kinds of drawing paper were all required and then purchased. A letter from the camp sent in February 1917 is to the Old Pencil Factory at Kidderminster possibly requesting the art material (Figure 4). A certain amount of Carbide was purchased; whether this was for a projector or additional lighting in the winter is not clear.

The text books cost £69.6.10d.(£69 34p), but some must have been sold on to students bringing in £35.11 2d (£35 56p).. Consumable material cost £26.17.4d (£26 87p). and there was a loss of £2 0. 9d (£2 4p) for nearly nineteen gallons of petrol that was either stolen or evaporated.

There is evidence from the accounts that either there were some students who were bad payers, or they did not have the ability to pay for their lectures and material; this loss accounted for £75 10 8d (£75 53p). Fortunately with the large number of students joining the courses some £438 19 6d (£438 97p) was available to the college and the losses could be borne.

With classes taking place in any of the three compounds during the day the internees needed a pass to go from one compound to another. Where there were many students attending the same class in another compound, a joint pass was issued with all their names on, which the authorities must have felt was simpler than issuing individual passes.

The college was divided into different faculties, namely Technical Science, Business Studies and Law, Natural Sciences which included Chemistry and Biology, Religion, English Prose, Modern German Literature and at least eleven New Languages that covered from English and French to Ukrainian and Arabic.

Other personnel covered book-keeping, preparing and reading balance sheets, office management, banking, aspects of different trade and economics.

Mr Held lectured on -

International Law- Is there still one in existence?

Public Law, in general.

Public Law with particular respect to the war, land war, naval war.

The powers and duties of neutral parties.

The opening ceremony was held

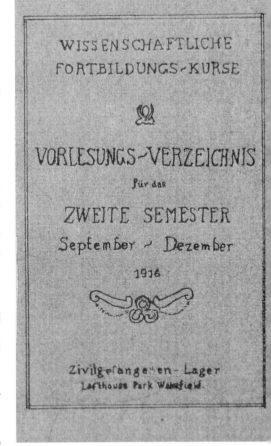

Figure 5. The timetable for the lectures during the second term, September to December 1916, at the civilian prison camp, Lofthouse Park.

with all due pomp on 1 October 1917 and lectures began the following day. The college operated for six days in the week, Monday to Saturday, from 10.30am to 4.45pm catering for the keen 651 internees who signed on to be students, by offering five periods each of forty-five minutes to a total of 140 hours. Over a third of the internee students took advantage of the introduced 'pound card' which enabled a student to attend all lectures. For students without any financial means it was made possible to apply for a free pass, but only five students fell into that category.

A booklet of lectures and their times was produced, hand written and drawn up for the Zweite Semester (Autumn term) but due to problems getting the schedules set out they were not ready until Christmas for the records and registers had to be typed out and possibly duplicated for the compounds where the courses were to be held (Figure 5). Records were kept showing the number of courses a

HANDELS- UND

RECHTSWISSENSCHAFTEN

I. Handelswissenschaften.

P. G r e v e:
   Buchfuehrung (Deutsche Buchhaltung)
   2 Std. Fri. 10.30-12.15 W.H.A. Beg. 20.Se

Dr. phil. F. S t e r n:
   Erlaeuterung von Bilanzen
   1 Std. Mi. 3 - 3.45 S.H. Beginn. 18.Sep

H. B e r l i n e r:
   Systematische Bureau Organisation
   1 Std. Mi. 4 - 4.45 S.H. Beginn: 2. Okt

Dipl.ing. M. F i e g e l:
   Kapitel der aussereuropaeischen Wirt-
   schaftsgeographie mit besonderer Be-
   ruecksichtigung technisch-wirtschaftl.
   cher Fragen.
   1 Std. Fri. 3-3.45 S.H. Beginn 25. Sept.

L. C l e m m:
   Die Bank im Dienste des Kaufmanns.
   1 Std. Mi. 11.30-12.15 W.H.A. Beg.18.Se

   Handelspraxis: Eine Reihe von Vortrae-
   gen ueber verschiedene Handelszweige
   und -Gebraeuche(Baumwollhandel, Kaffee-
   handel, Zuckerhandel etc.etc.)
   (Dozenten und Thema werden jeweils be-
   kannt gegeben)
   1 Std. Fri. 4 - 4.45 S.H.

Figure 6. Commerce and Law, list of lecturers and topics, showing, among others, P Greve offering German Accountancy on Friday mornings from 10.30am to 12.15pm, beginning on 20 September.

student had applied to attend and the number of times he did attend at each course (Figure 6).

When college reopened after the Christmas break the happy atmosphere of college life was disturbed by rumours of an exchange of internees, being negotiated from The Hague, which eventually happened with the transfer back to Germany of thirty-three of the lecturers (Figure 7). The lectures were continued, by re-jigging the courses and lecturers; these helped to get the students through the bouts of anticipation and disappointments. The College Principal, Professor Waetjen was one member to be selected for returning

Figure 7. A Christmas greeting sent by Hermann Held.

home, which created a problem with the administration of the college for his successor Dr Huelsenbeck, who continued as Head of Business Studies.

The finances of the college were strictly kept, with accounts of all incoming and outgoing transactions being noted with a profit and loss account and a balance sheet being produced, checked by Professor P Huelsenbeck and audited by F Merz, H Ostheide and H A Jordan. The term struggled on with the college closing officially on 30 March 1918 without any ceremony, but some courses continued until May as the lecturers had not completed their syllabuses in time.

A third semester was planned to run from January 1919 to the April but before then the civilian prisoners had all been transferred to the Isle of Man and it is now not clear if the term started.

For the rest of the year the remaining internees, and now there were some uniformed prisoners at the camp, worked at the increasingly important food-growing gardens and played games. The few who wanted to keep studying pooled their books together to make a library of 600 books which were kept in the South Camp. One hundred and thirty students paid the fee of three shillings (15p) per person, to belong to the library and borrow books. Students who had their course lecturer still with them at Lofthouse managed to start a new term but it was now a private study and unofficial.

This 'second term' began on 16 September 1918 with plans for the courses to extend into 1919 as many internees could not see an immediate return to Germany even if the war ceased in 1918. Due to modest capital being accumulated no fees were now charged for the lectures, but a sum of three shillings (15p) was charged for the identification card and pass. These could be obtained from Mr Morawski in the South Camp, Mr Kaiser in the West Camp and to the Office of Scientific further Education in the North camp.

With the surrender of large numbers of the German Armed Forces it became obvious that the authorities would need additional camps that had some security. Between 8 and 10 October 1918 the civilian prisoners at Lofthouse began to be transferred to Camp IV Knockaloe on the Isle of Man into Compound 4 which had been cleared of other inmates. This compound would be referred to as a 'Privilege Camp' for the new inmates had promised to pay eleven shillings (55p) per person every week for an improvement in rations, services, china and linens and they would be allowed to consume spirits, although this only went to drinking wine.

Life in the camp could have been more tolerable although many inmates may have been separated from their English relatives and friends. It would seem that the war was either over or nearly so, rehabilitation would soon be taking place and for the inmates from Wakefield there was much more entertainment in the camp along with lectures delivered by tutors such as Herman Held.

Wakefield internees had in the main to find their own physical,

Figure 8. A letter from one of the interness to the American Consulate in Manchester in 1915.

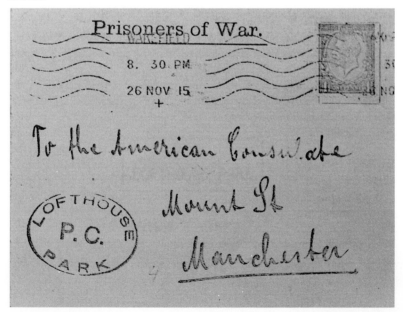

mental and recreative activities but at Knockaloe they were to find theatrical performances, concerts and talks on most nights.

People interested in Lofthouse Park may find more information through philately (Figure 8). There are several people in our area who have envelopes and postcards sent from Lofthouse Park during the period 1914-1919. Some of these 'notes' are sent to Germany or to places in Great Britain. One card had been sent to Gamages of London no doubt requesting some item to be sent from this department store, and another as already mentioned, to Kidderminster. A further letter in 1915 was sent to the American Consul at Manchester while another had been written to the London and South Western Bank. All these letters were written in English and would seem to have been communications to people that the writer had knowledge of. The sample the author has seen may be very small part of those written but the evidence seems to be overwhelmingly reinforcing the earlier description that the majority of people at Lofthouse Park were a privileged group.

Notes and References

1. In 1916 from a count taken after the sinking of the Lusitania there were 1,322 German civilians, 122 Austrians and Turks.
2. Dr Henning Ibs 25704 Meldorf
3. The sinking of this ship on 7 May 1815 helped to push America into the war as the ship carried many Americans amongst the 1,200 drowned passengers.
4. The German economic crisis was from 1929-33 when at one time wages were paid out daily to avoid further devaluation which was happening hourly.
5. The University of Freilburg refused to accept the records and coursework.

8. Some Mute Inglorious Milton

by Edward Green

AN AMERICAN'S DELUSIONS AND OBSESSION over a stately property in Wrenthorpe continued for over forty years. Battling against extreme poverty in his later years, Daniel Milton lived an odd existence, spending the little money he could earn on printing religious pamphlets airing his grievances against the leadership of the Christian Israelite Church. Wearing his Quaker-like clothes, he would carry a step ladder from his humble cottage along the Bradford Road to look over the high boundary walls onto Prophet Wroe's Mansion (Melbourne House) a property he believed was his by right (Figure 1). His hopeless quest to gain possession may have ended unfulfilled, but his life story is fascinating. Without doubt Milton was one of the most unusual characters to have lived in nineteenth century Wakefield.

Daniel Milton was born in October 1821 at Portsmouth, New Hampshire. His real name was Daniel Trickley and for many years he worked as a shipwright in New York. In his early twenties, Daniel became interested in the Millerite Church and in 1842 travelled throughout New England explaining the second coming of Christ. By the end of 1844 he was converted to another religious body, the Christian Israelites, a religion first taken to America in 1823 by two preachers sent over the Atlantic by Christian Israelite Leader, Yorkshireman John Wroe (1782-1863).

The Christian Israelite Church stemmed from the sect of Joanna

Figure 1. Melbourne House - Prophet Wroe's Mansion. *Vickers Orris.*

Southcott, a Devon servant who began receiving visions in 1792 and wrote many books of prophecies. Her fame spread and in the early 1800s she had many thousands of followers who waited eagerly when she predicted she would give birth to Shiloh the second Christ. Southcott died in December 1814, her promise unfulfilled after a *post mortem* revealed there was no sign of pregnancy. The Southcottian believers got round this major set back by saying that Shiloh had been born as a spirit and was taken up to heaven to reappear on earth in due course.

The sect continued for a time under the leadership of James Turner of Leeds, and, following his death in 1822, by Bradford born John Wroe who was to gain notoriety for his many travels, prophecies and behaviour. By 1830 he had been declared a 'Prophet' of the Church, but the most lasting legacy of Wroe in the Wakefield area is Melbourne House built at Brandy Carr, Wrenthorpe in 1856-7. A good outline history of Joanna Southcott and her successors is given in *Past Finding Out.*[1] Wroe's life story is covered by an entertaining account in Baring-Gould's *Yorkshire Oddities.*[2]

Milton's rise to power within the American arm of the Christian Israelite Church was rapid and he soon became a leading figure. In 1849 he was elected 'Judge' of the Christian Israelite Church in New York and he continued to make use of the title for the rest of his long life. In 1845 he had married a Scottish member of the sect, Barbara Kemp Williamson from Edinburgh, and the couple had three daughters. Milton's business prospered and in 1851 the Judge was instrumental in the establishment of the first Christian Israelite Sanctuary in America at number 108 First Street, New York.[3] He was made president and first trustee of the Church on 12 November of that year.

Daniel lived in Brooklyn in the 1850s and it was here that he met Prophet Wroe in 1854 on one of his four visits to America. Milton showed Wroe around the house he was building for himself after which Wroe told him 'Daniel, you will one day have another house built for you.' At the time Milton did not understand what Wroe meant by that strange prediction, but he began to interpret the meaning later that year, when Prophet Wroe announced he had received a command from the Lord to build a Temple.

Land was purchased at Brandy Carr, Wrenthorpe and funds for the project flooded in from the Prophet's credulous believers. The costly building was called Melbourne House because it was designed to resemble the old Town Hall at Melbourne, which Wroe would have seen on his third visit to Australia in 1854. Milton referred to the Melbourne House as the Christian Israelites' Temple, but in reality it is more like the wealthy Victorian gentleman's country residence. To this day locals call it Prophet Wroe's Mansion.

Melbourne House was formally opened at 3.00am on Whit Sunday 1857 attended by Christian Israelite delegates from all over the world. To his surprise, Daniel was not invited to the proceedings. The *Leeds Times* used the mansion's opening as an opportunity to carry two highly critical articles on Wroe and his followers. Milton was one of four prominent members of the Church in New York who wrote a strong letter of protest to the editor of the *Times*, dismissing the articles as 'calumny and unmitigated flagrant falsehoods.' They compared the articles in the *Leeds Times* with a favourable piece about the sect in an 1854 edition of the *New York Daily Times*. The Leeds paper never printed the letter, so the Christian Israelites published it themselves the following year at their Gravesend headquarters.

The co-writing of the *Leeds Times* letter appears to be one of the last acts Milton performed as a leader of the sect in America. For at about this time the bizarre obsession lodged in his mind that not only had Melbourne House been built for him according to his interpretation of Wroe's words, but also, more astonishingly he, Daniel Milton was the Promised Shiloh, the spiritual child of Joanna Southcott. Church members turned against him, his family left him, but Milton was resolved in his belief. As he explained in an interview towards the end of his life 'I am the child that was born at first as a spirit; and on 12 October 1821, I was born into the world in an ordinary way.'

Milton was convinced that Wroe's mission would end in November 1859 (forty years after Wroe's first vision). Daniel proclaimed his own mission in the *New York Sun* of 31 July 1858 and made his way to England the following year, to claim Melbourne House as his rightful inheritance. By the time he reached Wakefield in February 1860 Milton had just a farthing left in his pocket. He made his way to Melbourne House and confronted Wroe, quoting back the Prophet's words and stressing Wroe's ministry was over. Wroe rebuffed him, of course, and after many arguments a perplexed Milton went back to America.

Milton returned again the following year to again stake his claim to the mansion. Disturbances were frequent and Milton attempted to gain the support of believers and the public by staging a series of open-air meetings. These took place on Sunday afternoons and brought crowds of thousands of spectators who witnessed the Judge

Figure 2. The field opposite Melbourne House from which Milton preached.

preaching from an open cart. Daniel was soon in trouble however, for blocking the highway of Brandy Carr Road. Unperturbed, he hired a nearby field from Jane Ramsden, but the crowd of between six and seven thousand people who attended on 14 April again blocked the highway and Milton was taken to court by Wroe's lawyer, Wakefield solicitor Robert Barratt (Figure 2).

Milton's quarrel was not only with Prophet Wroe, but also with a fellow American John Laden Bishop. Bishop and his wife Margaret were Wroeite preachers who had accompanied Wroe on some of his travels and were probably responsible for converting Milton to the Christian Israelite faith. The Bishops preached at the Market Cross in Wakefield following the opening of Melbourne House and are often referred to in Wroe's books (Figure 3). The cause of the altercation according to Milton is that Bishop turned the New York congregation (including Milton's wife and children) against him. Milton frequently recounts a particular dispute with Bishop in the grounds of Melbourne House in May 1861. The police escorted Bishop back into the 'holy place' (the mansion), but Milton had another confrontation with Bishop later and 'broke his power by seizing hold of his long black beard.' Constable William Ramsden intervened and asked Bishop why he was keeping Milton's wife and children from him. The details of Bishop's hold over Milton's family are unclear, but we are informed that when Bishop died in 1866, Milton's wife paid for both his funeral expenses and a burial plot.

Another way in which Milton vented his grievances against Wroe was in the printing of handbills stating his claims. In August 1861

Figure 3. The market cross in Wakefield where the Bishops preached. *Wakefield Historical Publications.*

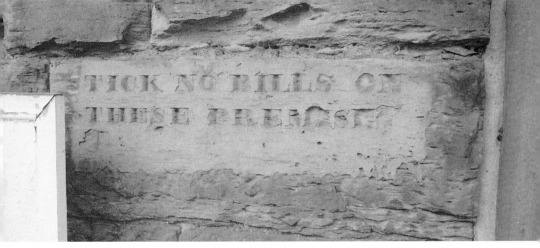

Figure 4. The prohibition - STICK NO BILLS - still to be seen on the perimeter wall at Melbourne House.

Milton again appeared in court at the Wakefield Petty Sessions, charged with doing wilful damage to the property of John Wroe – pasting handbills onto the high stone boundary walls of the mansion grounds. Wroe had previously warned Milton not to stick bills on his property and had gone to the trouble of carving a notice 'stick no bills on these premises' into one of the stones on the wall near the main gate (Figure 4). On 16 August Milton had been caught bill posting and was challenged by a visitor to Melbourne House who pointed out Wroe's notice. Daniel had continued sticking up his bills, saying the notice did not apply to him. The damage amounted to 6d (2.5p) which Milton was ordered to pay, plus 14s 6d (72.5p) expenses. Milton was threatened with fourteen days' imprisonment, but on this occasion the fine was paid. Soon after a frustrated Judge Milton again returned to the United States.

John Wroe died aged eighty, on 5 February 1863 whilst on a mission in Australia. The news did not reach Wakefield until the end of May and it eventually filtered through to the bewildered believers in America. On hearing of Wroe's death, Milton returned to England, determined to gain possession of the mansion. On 4 February 1864 he managed to gain entrance and claimed Melbourne House as church property holding it against a siege. Here he met a young servant Abby Eccles who told him she believed Wroe would return to the mansion when he had been dead for twelve months and was keeping the property ready for his return.

Milton held the mansion for almost a month, but was forced out on 1 March by a group led by the Deputy Chief Constable of the West Riding Constabulary and Wroe's lawyer. Days later, on 7 March 1864, John Wroe's will was proved. It had been drawn up by Barratt less than six months before the Prophet's death. The twelve page document offers a fascinating insight into the wealth of Prophet

Wroe, who left the majority of the estate to his grandson James.[4] This included not only Melbourne House and the neighbouring Melbourne House Farm in Brandy Carr Road, but also several cottages and parcels of land in the Wrenthorpe area. Wroe's three executors were prominent Christian Israelite Church members. Not surprisingly there is no mention of Milton in the entire document.

This did not deter Judge Milton who denounced Wroe's will as 'a villainous Church-swindling instrument.' In an article in *Yorkshire Life* magazine, January 1967, Prophet Wroe's great-grand-daughter, Marion Wroe[5] talked about her notorious ancestor and life at Melbourne House in the late nineteenth century. She described Milton as a man with flowing snow-white hair and recalled how he would follow her father James as he collected his weekly rent from his numerous tenants. Milton would wave his stick, shouting 'Do not pay this man. He's an impostor!'

The Judge took delight in any misfortune that befell the Wroe family and is said to have kept a list of all the deaths that occurred on the Wroe estate[6] since Milton's rejection by Prophet Wroe. There were constant skirmishes between him and members of the Wroe family, as well as workers on the estate. Prophet Wroe's second son Joseph lived at Carr Gate a couple of doors away from the *Malt Shovel*. He threatened Milton several times and on one occasion got a gang of men from the pub to drive him away from the gates of Melbourne House. The Judge was frequently pelted with stones and clods of earth and had buckets of 'dirty water' thrown over him. Only days before his death one of the Wroes turned a hose onto Milton as he walked by the gates of the mansion.

Like Prophet Wroe before him, the more Judge Milton was persecuted, the more this determined his resolve. The sacrifices he made for his deluded belief were immense: his wife and family, his business and his comfortable home in the United States; and all because he believed he was the promised Shiloh and had the futile hope of possession of Wroe's mansion. Again, like Wroe, Milton was of the strange belief that he would never die.

By the 1870s, Daniel had settled into an odd pattern of travel between England and America in his attempts to assert his claim to Melbourne House and gain leadership of the Christian Israelite Church. He lived in a cottage at Woolstone Nook which neighboured the grounds of the mansion. When this cottage was demolished, he moved to another at Wilson Hill on the northern side of the Bradford Road. This row of houses survives and has been converted into the Poplars Guest House (Figure 5). Here he was happy (according to

Figure 5. Poplars Guest House in 2001. In one of the cottages, subsequently converted into the guest house, Daniel Milton lived in the 1870s.

one contemporary account), as many of his neighbours were Christian Israelites too. In fact the terrace was known locally as 'Joanna Row'. Milton appears to have lived in at the very least two other properties, both in a row of late Victorian red brick houses known as Springfield View[7] at Bragg Lane End.

Figure 6. Cover of a collection of pamphlets issued by Daniel Miton in 1890. *Wakefield Library Headquarters, Local Studies collection.*

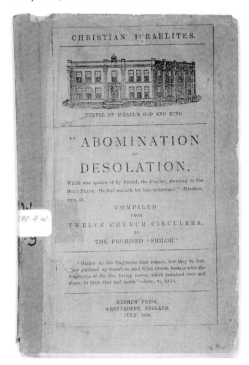

In Milton's visits to his native country he travelled sometimes as a paying passenger, sometimes working his passage. The voyage to America was not of course without its dangers. He is said to have been almost shipwrecked twice in the two dozen times he made the trip. On one journey across the Atlantic, Milton's ship was struck by a storm and developed a leak. When the water in the hold had reached the depth of six feet, a sailor cried out that the vessel was sinking. A scornful Judge looked on observing, 'Never while Daniel Milton is on board.' Apparently it was largely due to his exertion that the ship was saved.[8]

Milton subsisted by undertaking various jobs, such as carpentry, painting, white-washing and making items on his joiner's bench. When funds permitted, he issued pamphlets from what he called the 'Hebrew Press' at Wrenthorpe (Figure 7). When in America he issued similar pamphlets from the 'Hebrew Press' at an address in New York. In April 1876 his Wrenthorpe office was raided by the police and the printing press thrown out onto the street. Milton's publications had titles such as 'The Millennial Educator', 'The Believer's Manifesto' and 'The Perfect Gospel Advocate.' Indeed in the 1881 Census returns, Milton appears to make a particularly bold claim, even for him. Then aged fifty-nine he described himself as the Editor and Publisher of the Eternal Gospel. This however turns out to be the title of yet another of Milton's publications. In 1891 he describes his occupation as Christian Israelite Minister.

Three letters from Milton to George Horridge a Wakefield printer and publisher of the *Wakefield Almanack* survive.[9] The first, dated 17 September 1872 arranges for his goods to be shipped back to Portsmouth, New Hampshire and tells how he had spent the summer working at his brother's farm to pay off all his debts. The two other letters are of ten years later and mention the mansion.[10] Writing from Ayres, Mass., 28 January 1882, Milton says how he had been anxious to obtain a photograph or engraving of Melbourne House, but had failed and concluded it was

not for me to get one, as it will only be a shadow, and what do I want of a shadow when I get in Melbourne House and have the substance.

The next part of the letter is very moving. Milton writes about visiting the grave of his eldest daughter who had recently died and four other children who had presumably died in infancy.

There are now five of our

Figure 7. A page from the 1890 collection of pamphlets. *Wakefield Library Headquarters, Local Studies collection.*

CHURCH CIRCULAR, NUMBER TWO.

MELBOURNE HOUSE—HOUSE OF ISRAEL.

MURDEROUS!

From the *Wakefield Express*, June 10, 1871.

JUDGE MILTON
BEFORE THE MAGISTRATES AGAIN.

Yesterday, at the West Riding Police Court, before Mr. S. G. Leatham and Major Barker, Daniel Milton, who styles himself as "Judge" Milton, affirming that he is the duly-appointed Judge in the "Christian Israelite Church," was summoned for doing damage to the property of John Buckley and William Farrand, by posting placards on gate-posts on their property.

As many of our readers are aware, contiguous to Wakefield, on the Wakefield and Bradford road, and situate on a commanding eminence, is a magnificent building, known generally as "Prophet Wroe's Mansion," and more properly designated "Melbourne House," and which, with the farm adjacent, is tenanted by Mr. John Buckley. This building was erected some years ago, by the followers of the late Joanna Southcott. For a time the "Prophet" resided at the "Mansion," which was opened in the presence of thousands of people, hailing from various parts of the world. On his decease the property fell into the hands of certain trustees, of whom Mr. Farrand, of Ashton-under-Lyne, is one. Milton, who is an American shipwright, claims to be the rightful successor of the late "Prophet," and, believing that the Mansion was erected out of the funds of the Church, maintains his claim to be considered the owner, in trust, until the departed Founder, or the late "Prophet"—we forget which—shall re-visit this sublunary sphere. Announcing himself as "The Promised Shiloh," he has not ceased, in season and out of season, by tongue and pen—he publishes a periodical called "The Revelator"—to put forth his claims. Several times has he been in gaol for *children... in Cypress Hills Cemetery with their Christian Names only on their gravestones. No one would know but they were all John Bishop's children, as he lies buried in the midst of them, and on his stone is pronounced a tender parent, when he never begot a child in his life.*

It is a very strange state of affairs which is never properly explained. The poignancy however, soon gives way to the usual ranting, for within a sentence we read:

But she [Milton's wife] *will see better days with me in Melbourne House. If the Ashton Tribe discard James Wroe's right to the property, what position are they in? Will they not be brought face to face with me? Remember I told thee they would come at the Last and bow at my feet. What they have caused me to suffer knows no one but myself.*

Figure 8. Part of a letter written by John Whiteley to Daniel Milton in 1893. *Wakefield Library Headquarters, Local Studies collection.*

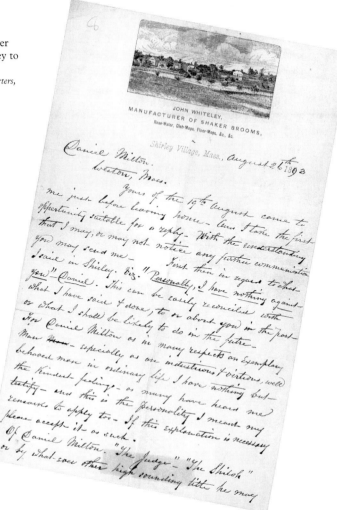

In the 1890s, Milton decided to stay in England as bouts of ill health and perpetual poverty had somewhat curtailed his travel. By this time he had descended still further into religious obscurity and isolation. In 1888 he had failed in his appeal to lead the Christian Israelite community at Gillingham, Kent following the death of their leader Jezreel (James White) and his widow Queen Esther (Clarissa Rogers). There is also evidence that he tried to join a Shaker community in America. A surviving letter[11] from John Whiteley a leading light of the Shaker community of Shirley Village, Masseuses, rejects Milton's unconventional approach to lead the sect that he made on a visit to the States in 1893 (Figure 8). Milton seems to have barged into Whiteley's shop, claiming that the Lord had sent him to take over the management of the Shaker community. Whiteley's reply was swift, namely that the Lord had said nothing to him on the subject.

The 1890s also saw the death of Milton's wife Barbara in America in 1893. Although they had been separated for over thirty-five years, Milton wrote to her frequently, desperately asking her to come back. All his appeals were ignored. Of the rest of Milton's family in the United States, a nephew actually was a judge. Milton supposedly said to him 'You are a judge of the temporal courts, but I am a judge of the eternal courts.'

The local media took a fascination in Milton's character, with several articles about the Judge, dubbed the Prophet of Potovens[12] by one paper. In the interviews his religious frenzy continued with Milton repeatedly insisting that he was the promised Shiloh, 'Joanna Southcott's spiritual son' who was (according to the Judge) 'foretold by Jacob.'

As well as his religious beliefs, the press also gave coverage of Milton's unconventional life style, in particular his vegetarian diet. Daniel had given up eating meat as a young man and from that age to his death he was also a non-smoker and drank nothing but cold water. In his latter years this meagre diet became essential because of his poverty and it was said locally that he survived on swede and cabbage. In an interview in the *Manchester Guardian* 22 December 1899, he tells of a typical day's meals:

> For breakfast I generally have boiled beans and toast. For dinner I have pea-flour – you can make a pint of excellent soup with two tablespoons of pea-flour, and it improves it to add some breadcrumbs. My third and last meal is supper – sometimes bread and water, sometimes pea-flour.

The articles also describe his meagre living room with its bare stone floor, old-fashioned hand printer, boxes of type, bundles of literature and heaps of books. There were no blinds or curtains at the windows of his cottage. Instead the Judge pinned old newspapers to the window frames to keep out both the draught and the prying eyes of passers by. Above the mantelpiece the following was printed in large letters:

Jesus and Joanna
My two witnesses
Shiloh

The output of religious pamphlets continued when funds permitted. One of Milton's appeals, published in the local press in late 1890s begins with the wonderful lines 'Sir, it is no disgrace to be poor, but it is very inconvenient.' In his appeals he rails against his many oppressors: magistrates, solicitors, the police, the Home Secretary all of whom failed to help his cause. He even criticises the newly formed Stanley Urban District Council for charging rates to a poor old man.

Milton found himself in the news again at the turn of the twentieth century, following eviction from his cottage for rent arrears. The octogenarian spent a night sleeping by the side of the Bradford Road guarding his possessions and was forced to sell many items including his carpenter's tools to find rent for a neighbouring cottage.

Judge Milton vigorously pursued his claims to Melbourne House right up until the very week of his death. On Monday, 14 December 1903, a delighted Milton managed to get hold of a key to one of the lodges of Melbourne House. A local policeman Constable Lindley was called and eventually persuaded Milton to give it back. Constable Lindley heard Milton the following evening as he walked along the Bradford Road past the Judge's cottage. He said he often heard the Judge talking and singing at night.

On the Wednesday of that week a neighbour, Mrs Elizabeth Ball, grew worried, as she had not seen Milton around that day. She peeped through a gap in the newspapers covering the windows and saw Daniel lying on the floor at the bottom of the stairs leading to the kitchen. She sought assistance to break into his cottage where 'Shiloh' was found lying unconscious, his head cut and bruised. Milton never regained consciousness and died the following day. At the inquest into his death, held at the *Wheel* P H, Bragg Lane End on Saturday 19 December a verdict of accidental death was returned.

Milton appears to have been respected by local villagers in Wrenthorpe. Perhaps this was because of their unease towards the Wroes. Their respect for the aged almost patriarchal figure was however, not as great as their pity. One account of Milton's death states that 'the villagers are touched with sadness that so sturdy and kindly a creature should have lived and died in such a pitiable cause'.[13]

Milton's funeral took place on Monday, 21 December 1903. About a dozen people attended and local villagers contributed £2 towards the costs. The coffin was interred at Alverthorpe Churchyard by Reverend C P Mellor. Surely this curate would never again bury such an unusual religious figure in his entire career.

Notes and References

1. Balleine, G R (1956) *Past Finding Out: The Tragic Story of Joanna Southcott and her Successors.* London: SPCK.
2. Baring-Gould, Rev S (1900) *Yorkshire Oddities, Incidents and Strange Events.* (Reprinted by Smith Settle, Otley, 1987).
3. The building was later used as a Jewish Synagogue.
4. Wroe outlived his eldest son Benjamin. James Wroe was a dairy farmer at Melbourne House Farm. He died in March 1919 aged sixty-six and is buried in Alverthorpe Churchyard with his wife Sarah.
5. The second eldest daughter of James Wroe. She died aged ninety-two in December 1969.
6. Reminiscent of the footnotes in Wroe's books relating to the fates that befell named individuals who had crossed him.
7. Built in the 1890s, this terrace survives and is now numbered 345-351 Bradford Road; although the end two houses which included the house where Milton died (No. 353) were unfortunately demolished in about 1970.
8. Article in Cuttings Book, Ref. 42/263 at Balne Lane Library, Wakefield.
9. Horridge was in business in Wood Street, Wakefield from about 1849-91 and also printed material for Goodwyn Barmby, the founder of the Communist Church.
10. I am grateful to Daphne Cross of Brampton, Ontario for copies of these letters.
11. In the local history collection at Balne Lane Library, ref. Box 4f.
12. The alternative name for Wrenthorpe, originating from the post-medieval pottery industry that once thrived there.
13. *Yorkshire Post*, 19 December 1903, p.7.

Primary Sources

1. Copy of a letter addressed to the Editor of the *Leeds Times* by the Christian Israelite Church in the United States of America. Published Gravesend, 1858. British Library Shelfmark 4139.d.95.
2. John Wroe's Will, proved 7 March 1864.
3. Census returns for Stanley-cum-Wrenthorpe township, 1871, 1881 and 1891.
4. *Twelve Church Circulars* compiled by Daniel Milton, 1890. Balne Lane Library, Wakefield, Ref. 289.9W.
5. Late nineteenth century newspaper articles in cuttings books at Balne Lane Library Wakefield, Ref. 36/34, 36/38 42/235, 42/255, 42/262, 42/264, 42/327, 42/363, 42/369, 88/198, 89/134.
6. Letter to Daniel Milton from Shaker John Whitely, ref. Box 4f. Balne Lane Library.
7. *Wakefield Express* 24 Aug 1861; 5 July 1879; 19 Dec 1903; 26 Dec 1903.
8. Three letters from Milton to George Horridge, dated 17 Sep 1872, 28 Jan 1882 and 24 Nov 1882.
9. *Manchester Guardian* 22 December 1899.
10. *Yorkshire Post* 19 December 1903.
11. *Yorkshire Evening Post* 18 December 1903.
12. Alverthorpe Church Burial Records, County Records Office, Wakefield Ref. D43/12.
13. *Yorkshire Life* magazine, January 1967.

Secondary Sources

1. Roger, P G (1963) *The Sixth Trumpeter: The Story of Jezreel and his Tower.* Oxford University Press, p.97.
2. Harrison, J F C (1979) *The Second Coming: Popular Millenarianism 1780-1850.* London: Routledge & Kegan Paul Ltd. Footnote, p.254.

9. Hilltop, Hillside and Riverside, The Story of Three Adjacent but Differing Medieval Townships: Chevet, Walton and Sandal

by John Goodchild

Introduction

THREE ADJOINING CENTRAL WEST RIDING TOWNSHIPS, disparate in almost every way, Walton, Sandal and Chevet, were in two different parishes, three manors, and two wapentakes; they possessed differing landowning patterns, their areas quite markedly varied, as did their population sizes. One, Sandal Magna, was a township comprising a number of small hamlets; Walton had but one major settlement, with two nearby hamlets and another abandoned in the Middle Ages; the third, Chevet, was a single-village township whose freeholds were ultimately bought out and the village itself destroyed.

But the survival of a large collection of medieval deeds in the writer's Collection, 146 in number and relating principally to the fourteenth century – although a number are earlier and some later too - enables some conclusions to be drawn and some hypotheses set up in relation to these three contiguous townships, Walton, Sandal and Chevet, which lie to the south of the river Calder. Other deed collections, especially those printed in the Yorkshire Archaeological Society's volumes of *Yorkshire Deeds*, and the Newland manuscript which are also in the author's collection, enable the study to be widened and various conjectures more closely examined. A number of really significant factors emerge: the scale of small freeholder landowners, recognisable elsewhere in the locality, can here be studied in some depth, along with freehold and copyhold joint landowning, and landowning in more than one township; the establishment of medieval village chapels; population movement, now obviously remarkable by the fourteenth century; the changing names of local enclosures and of the parts of the open fields, rather than of field names fossilised from antiquity; the local reaction to support for the later Crusades; the possibility of the existence of a small sub-freeholder class, whose names appear only as witnesses to deeds; the occasions for the 'loss' of hamlets; the very character of some of the personalities recorded in the deeds. These and some other matters are considered in this study.

The topographical situation

The three townships of Sandal Magna, Walton and Chevet succeed each other topographically in an ascent of the southern valley wall of the Calder, rising from sixty foot or so above sea level at the lowest part of Sandal at Fall Ing to some 300ft near Chevet Hall. The soils are congenial to agriculture, and overlie the coal measures; coalmining is an ancient industry in Walton township, and the Chevet Rock is a major source of building stone. These three vills are watered and drained by a number of streams, which rise beyond their boundaries and flow through them: one, running down from Notton with the names variously of Bleakley Dike and Owler Beck, forms the western boundary of both Chevet and Sandal townships and passes through Newmillerdam lake, dropping into the Calder at Porto Bello near Wakefield; the other, with tributaries including the Bull Bridge Dike, rises near Wintersett and runs through Walton Park lake before becoming Drain Beck and Oakenshaw Beck. It forms the eastern boundary of Sandal and joins the Calder below Heath Common. In fact, streams form a large part of the boundaries of all three townships, except where the boundaries necessarily follow higher land.

The three townships are very different in their settlement patterns. Sandal comprises a number of small hamlets rather than one major village: Sandal itself, Milnthorpe, Standbridge, Woodthorpe, Hilltop and Newbiggin, Pledwick, Agbrigg, Sandal Castle, Little Sandal, and Manygates. Walton, on the other hand, consisted of one village with two nearby hamlets, known as Middle Walton (or generally as Walton), Lower Walton or Lower Town, and Upper Walton or Overtown, with the addition of the hamlet(?s) of Woodhouse and/or Woodsome, probably abandoned at or before the Black Death. Chevet was one village, but was described in 1517 as deserted: as we shall see, one owning family had over a long period inherited from, or bought out, others.

Sandal village lay close to but just off a major north to south road route through Yorkshire, now the A61, although now on a different alignment. The old main road passed from Wakefield Bridge End – to which it is aligned, possibly significantly, along Manygates Lane and apparently on via Chevet Lane, close to the Walton boundary at two points, and through Chevet. Suggestively, Gallows Hill is traversed by this road (Figure 1). A subsidiary road, which may have been a predecessor to the present road from Wakefield to Doncaster, left the former road at Little Sandal and initially (now as Castle Road) formed the southern boundary back lane of the medieval hamlet of Sandal before passing on to Walton and thence to Crofton; an alternative to this road was to use the main road and then turn at what is now Walton Station Lane. The suffix lane nearly always argues for the existence of an old road.

In the case of Sandal, the building of a new line of road in the mid-eighteenth century between the *Three Houses* and Manygates, cutting through the medieval village on a line differing from the old axis, which was

Figure 1. Gallows Hill. *Kate Taylor.*

apparently parallel to the back lane, now Castle Road, results in the alignment of the older surviving houses of today being different from that of the present main road – which on its new line avoided narrow stretches, bends and steep hills (Figure 2). Both Sandal and Walton were gable-end-to-street villages, a situation some evidence of which remains today on the ground: a more clear local example survives in

Figure 2. Houses at Sandal on an alignment different from the present main road.

Figure 3. Barleywood House. *Kate Taylor.*

the village of Warmfield nearby. At Sandal, some early Victorian houses still followed the old frontage axis; the old village is terminated in the north by Barleywood House, a seventeenth century structure which has an old alignment, but runs parallel to it in its axis

Figure 4. The area of the well at Sandal, reorganised in 1845 and partially repaired by Wakefield Historical Society in 2001. *Kate Taylor.*

(Figure 3). The Sandal axis is roughly NW/SE, that of Walton SW/NE, and Walton shows no evidence of any single boundary back lane, although many local villages, like Sandal, do so: Warmfield and Crigglestone are two examples. Both Sandal and Walton were located where an adequate water supply presumably formed one important locational factor: at Sandal the early Victorian reorganisation of the public troughs, fed from a shallow well, survives intact with the date 1845 (Figure 4). In each case, too, there are unfilled housing sites, apparently never filled, suggesting an original planned layout in both cases, with an incomplete takeup of sites – a layout more extensive than demand called for. Many of these sites, without any indication of ever having been used – although archaeological excavation might be necessary to test for the remains of wooden buildings which had disappeared as, for example, the population decreased rapidly after the visitation of a medieval outbreak of plague - such sites remained to take dateable Georgian and later buildings, or in the case of a long strip of land behind the War Memorial at Walton, the land is still unoccupied.

Administrative contrasts
In almost every administrative way too, Sandal, Walton and Chevet differed. Size-wise, Chevet was a small township of but 839 acres, while Sandal was almost twice that size with 1620 acres, and Walton, larger still, had some 1820 acres. Chevet lay in the Wapentake of Staincross while Walton and Sandal were in that of Agbrigg, itself the name of one of the hamlets (and of a bridge) within Sandal township. Chevet was in the great medieval Honour of Pontefract and was split at an early stage among a number of major, as well as a variety of minor, landholdings. Chevet seems never to have had a working manorial system, or at least no references to its court or to copyhold tenures have been found. Sandal was within the great Manor of Wakefield and held in hand or demesne by its lord, while Walton was in the same manor of Wakefield but a part of Walton (perhaps rather than the whole) was created (or subinfeudated) as the Manor of Walton, courts for which manor continued until the last was held in 1852. In Sandal there were extensive areas of Manor of Wakefield copyhold (and freehold) properties, in Walton apparently no copyholds held of either Walton or Wakefield manors although the Hospitallers' Manor of Newland encompassed properties in Walton given as pious gifts – or possibly to purchase freedom from a certain time in post-mortal purgatory – to that religious body, just as Newland Manor had properties also in Sandal

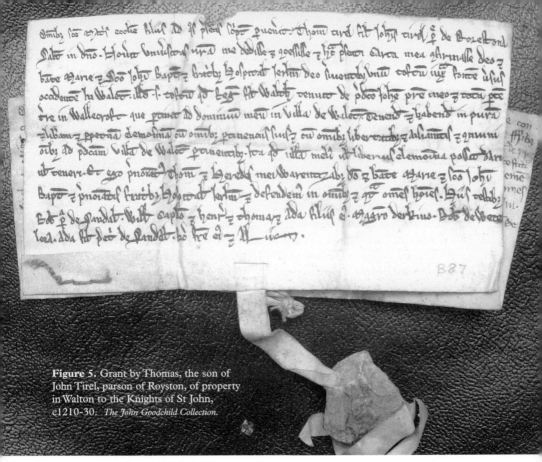

Figure 5. Grant by Thomas, the son of John Tirel, parson of Royston, of property in Walton to the Knights of St John, c1210-30. *The John Goodchild Collection.*

and Milnthorpe (Figure 5).

Ecclesiastically, Chevet was a township within Royston parish, while Walton and Sandal were in that of Sandal: in medieval times, but not later, both Walton and Chevet had for some time their own chapels of ease, each served by a chaplain (Figure 6). Administratively, Sandal remained independent until 1909 when it was absorbed into the slowly-growing municipal borough of Wakefield, while Walton and Chevet remained parishes within rural districts until local government reorganisation in 1974.

Some relevant details survive which allow comparisons to be made between these three townships, albeit the bases of the figures are very different.

	1379 Poll Tax Heads of Families	1672 Hearth Tax Hearths	1801 census Families
Walton	24	60	67
Sandal	32	60	169
Chevet	12	1	10

Figure 6. Sandal Church.
Wakefield Historical Publications.

Chevet had come to be in late medieval times, through both marriage and buying-up from other freeholders, a one-owner township, with a hall and (though probably only later) a couple of outlying tenanted farms (one such existed in 1641) but in Sandal, despite numerous purchases from larger and smaller owners of both freehold and copyhold properties, by 1879 the Chevet Hall Pilkingtons owned only some 520 acres in Sandal (or about one third of the township's area). In Walton, both Pilkingtons and the resident Waterton family of Walton Hall, an estate they had acquired through marriage in 1435, owned by the 1870s over 80 percent of Walton between them, after heavy buying, and the Pilkingtons owned the whole of Chevet (Figure 7).

In all three cases, areas of land were cultivated by the time of the *Domesday Book* of 1086: four carucates in Chevet, with six acres of pasturable wood, six carucates in Sandal and eight in Walton. In 1297 taxation was laid upon Walton and Sandal on the following basis:

	horses	oxen	cows	sheep	qrs oats	qrs wheat	heads of livestock	qtrs of grain
Sandal	5	4	4	10	19	2	23	21
Walton	6	6	6	16	14	4.5 plus six bushels	34	4.5?

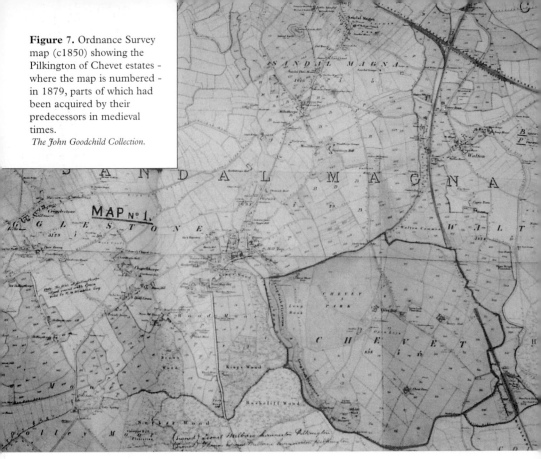

Figure 7. Ordnance Survey map (c1850) showing the Pilkington of Chevet estates – where the map is numbered – in 1879, parts of which had been acquired by their predecessors in medieval times.

The John Goodchild Collection.

Sheep farming in Walton is mentioned in the deed collections under review, while Chevet, whose wapentake had not been included in the surviving 1297 returns, had a sheepfold for 30 sheep in about 1250, built on the site of a house and croft formerly of one Cutta. Chevet was ultimately to cease to be as a village as a result of clearance of its houses, after their purchase, for a sheep walk, between 1485 and 1517.

Reference can usefully be made here to the other lost village, that of Woodsome, or Woodhouse, (were they one or two communities?) which lay within Walton township but apparently at some distance from the group of hamlets called Walton. Woodhouse probably lay beyond the present Walton Hall park: between c1180 and 1210, Adam, son of Aldred of Woodhouse gave to the Hospitallers an acre in Upper Santingley with rights belonging to the village of Woodhouse, and at a similar period the same Adam gave to the Hospitallers lands in the field of Woodhouse called Hug Rode, lying between his father's lands and that of Henry Prudfoot. In a deed of c1202-1210, Adam, who now describes himself as of Woodhouse, gives six acres there for the salvation of the souls of himself, his father, mother and all his ancestors, with common pasture pertaining to the vill of Woodhouse. It is not clear as to what became of this land, and it is not the property of the Hospitallers in 1539-40, the mid-sixteenth century. The surname de Woodhouse survives only until the later fourteenth century among the surviving deeds, after which no references occur to the name as either a surname or a place name. On the other hand the name Heghrod, mentioned as a place in one of the grants to the Hospitallers, survived as a family name in the Poll Tax of 1379 and in deeds as late as 1400.

The actual layout of the three townships in medieval times is illustrated by the descriptions of properties being sold, gifted (in marriage or to relatives), exchanged or tenanted – often by a man and his wife - although in the absence of maps before 1800 in the cases of Walton and Sandal, and before 1825 in the case of Chevet, it is impossible to correlate the actual medieval situation on the ground with the modern one.

Chevet was the only township or vill of the three with a nucleated village at its heart. In medieval Chevet, some at least of the houses had their own names: Olive Yard in 1317, Monk Place in 1404, Marget Place, described in 1432 as being in the middle of the town. In 1485 one property in Chevet consisted of a house, a garden and adjoining croft; one was described in 1317 as being a capital messuage, a term (at least later) usually betokening a substantial house. The farmlands belonging to individual owners' dwellings – not by any means always stated – varied considerably: in 1302 and again in 1342 a house and its bovate of land are mentioned – an area which could be ploughed by an ox in a year, from some ten to eighteen acres (others suggest seven to thirty-two acres), alternatively known as an oxgang. In 1313 a Chevet property consisted of a house and sixteen acres and half an acre of meadow land; in 1325 of a house, buildings and seventeen and a half acres of arable; in 1375 of a house and thirteen acres – all of which might suggest a median average of some fourteen acres. Up to 1432, some land was still described as an assart – as newly made clearing from the waste, now brought into cultivation. The village possessed at least one orchard in c1300; it was surrounded by strip fields, named as the South, the East, the West (in 1287), the Middle and the Kirk (or?) Chapel Fields, themselves divided into strips, lands or swathes, two of which in c1300 contained an acre in Chevet, while in another instance three strips, or selions, covered half an acre. The chapel of Chevet, mentioned in 1286, was separated from the town by arable land.

Sheepfarming was important: in 1240 reference is made to building a sheepfold for up to 300 sheep, and in 1287 to a ditched sheepfold and pasture for up to 200 sheep. There was a town green mentioned in 1317, a common in 1252. Rents were payable and sometimes silver is mentioned, and occasionally there is a reference to compulsory work - mowing and ploughing in autumn, or two men mowing and ploughing for fifteen days in the year. In 1485 a nominal rent of a red rose was payable in August, and in 1287 reference is made to a villein being reserved from a twenty-year lease of Chevet property; his name was Robert Leueriche.

Chevet had its own powered cornmilling system on the stream which flows down from Notton and on through Newmillerdam; about 1300 there is a reference to an assart in Chevet towards the mill of Notton and to the road leading to the watermill of Chevet; another undated deed of a similar period refers to the North Mill, one of 1348 to the Mill Well. Both Walton and Sandal possessed such powered facilities too. A Chevet deed of 1641 refers to the Milne Cliffe wood and meadow in Chevet, and the present topography of the valley suggests where these presumably three mills were located.

The medieval Chevet deeds enable one to trace the initial modest landownership in the village of the humble Monk family from 1314 through both additional land purchases and marriages, through the Bosvile (to 1515) and Nevile families (to 1765) when it passed by purchase for the first time to the closely related Pilkington family who owned it until 1951.

One particular point of signficance is the manner in which the surviving deeds illustrate the local mobility in the medieval period. People moved a lot. Immigration and presumably emigration were considerable and continuous, as illustrated by the transfers of property, although nothing seems to be shown of the local effects of the Black Death in the middle years of the fourteenth century. The name of John Bradley (Huddersfield?) is certainly that of an incomer in the purchase of property: doubtless he was of once-Flemish extraction. He acquired land in Walton in 1399-1400. Numbers of landowners owned property in a variety of townships, and landholding in Sandal and Walton together seems to have been relatively common. Field names changed too: of the hundreds of field names in a survey of Walton in 1841, for example, only three are common to 1841 and the many recorded medieval field names of that township.

The deeds themselves are of course in Latin, and they are almost all undated until well into the fourteenth century, when first regnal years and then dates according to the Christian calendar – 1340, 1357, 1389 etc – are mentioned in them.

Land holdings varied enormously in their size, and in many instances the small freeholder must have found difficulty in achieving a livelihood from the land which he owned himself, doubtless thus having to rent land from the old, from those unable to work it and/or from spinsters or widows or, indeed, from absentees. Even the craftsman appears to have owned agricultural land in strips and closes, which no doubt he worked himself as a smallholding, or let. There is also the unresolved question of the employment status of unmarried women. Did the women who bought or acquired land, farm it themselves? Why were there numbers of women described as, eg. Matild, daughter of Adam Carpenter of Walton and Margaret her daughter (1356), or a grant made by the three daughters of Matild daughter of Peter de Walton (of 1310-11)? Men and wives granted land together, and a wife grants alone, not being particularly specified as a widow. Another aspect of the story relates to the serfs belonging to even the small tenants. Their exact status is unknown, but they do just occasionally surface, in that they and their families and goods are part of a conveyed property, or that they are specifically conveyed, particularly, but perhaps not exclusively, as a gift to a religious house.

In Walton the ownership structure changed from one of a considerable number of small freeholders and the larger owner of the Walton Hall estate, to one where from the middle of the seventeenth century the freeholds were bought up on an increasing scale by the Neviles and subsequently by their successors as owners of the Chevet Hall estate, the Pilkingtons, who in 1879 owned 473a 0 25p in Walton, being some twenty-five per cent of the area of the township while the Waterton estate was one of 951 acres (ie c396a, or twenty-two per cent of the land remained in other freeholder hands).

In Sandal, despite further Nevile and Pilkington purchases again over a long period, and their ultimate acquisition of over 520 acres, numbers of freeholders remained (1100 acres or about sixty per cent of the total being freeholds or copyholds) and in both Sandal and Walton the Pilkingtons began ultimately in Victorian times to sell off villa sites.

In Chevet the situation was quite different, for there the whole of the acreage of the township was owned apparently by the Bosviles of Chevet by 1485, the date of their last recorded purchase in the surviving deeds, from whom the Chevet estate passed by marriage to Sir John Nevile, who rebuilt Chevet Hall in 1529. He it was who apparently caused the removal of the village of Chevet, and perhaps the removal of its chapel, if that had so long survived. Nevile claimed to have undertaken all his work at Chevet since c1508, including the building of a fence around the park. One farm existed there, apart from the mansion, in 1641: subsequently, as is still the case, there were two farms but the population of Chevet at the time of the first national census, that of 1801, was only seventy-five including the servants in and about the hall; in 1991 it was thirty-five.

The medieval situation in neighbouring Walton was quite different in a number of ways, but principally in that no one owning family ever achieved complete ownership of the township, and as late as the nineteenth century there remained numbers of small freeholders there, along with the medievally established Waterton family of Walton Hall (who had derived their estate in 1435 by marriage from the de Burghs), and the Pilkingtons of Chevet Hall who had, over the centuries from the sixteenth, bought up pieces of land there. The ancient deeds of the Watertons and their predecessors appear to have disappeared, but the survival of the deeds of the Pilkington and predecessor estate in Walton enables some detail of medieval Walton to be identified.

A taxation list for Walton of 1297 (such a return does not survive for Chevet) shows a primarily agricultural economy, as one would anticipate, although without the marked emphasis on sheepfarming of Chevet and perhaps, judging from the relatively small numbers of oxen, one more pastoral than crop-growing. Analysed, the 1297 listing shows:

Name	Horses	Oxen	Cows	Heifers	Sheep
Richard King	1	0	2	0	10
William Witbelt	1	1	1	0	0
Robert son of Henry	1	0	1	1	6
William Watti	1	1	1	1	0
Bate son of Hugh	1	2	1	0	0
William Grave	1	1	0	0	0

wheat and oats were the produce of all these holdings, and numbers of deeds survive in relation to a number of these men and their families and successors, especially to the Kings and Witbelts, whose estates came together into the hands of the King family through the marriage settlement of c1300 which is so unusual a survival of this period. The Poll Tax returns of 1379 list the names of twenty-four families in Walton: some with the wife's name, some of single men and women, one a daughter, another a mother, three of servants (with their masters named); all were charged at the standard 3d (1.5p) and only two occupations are listed, both blacksmiths. The Manor of Walton was held as a sub-manor of that of Wakefield and by the de Burgh family of Walton Hall; no medieval records of manorial jurisdiction appear to have survived, although there are records of later court leet (ie no copyhold properties) jurisdiction existing from 1579, apart from those of the medieval manor of Newland, where properties had been given to aid the maintenance of the Crusades in the Holy Land from as early as c1180 to 1210 by gifts from Adam son of Aldred of Woodhouse near Walton, and by Thomas son of John Tirel parson of Royston in c1210 to 1230. The latter gift was described as being in part a toft, or house place, in Walton near the well there, the former being at Woodhouse (as it was earlier called, later referred to as Woodsome), a hamlet in Walton towards Santingley and now a lost village. The medieval deeds refer to Middle Walton from 1347 and to Woodhouse hamlet from about 1210; they allude only to the North Field of Walton as a strip field, but also refer to Walton Common, to the Moors, the great meadow with swaiths in it - and to many now quite unidentifiable field names with divided areas within them. A deed of 1321-22 mentions land between the bridges of Walton, and an undated one of c1300 mentions a rent of a cock at Christmas, along with a mention in c1314 of Robert son of the Reeve. One of 1408 is a thirty-year lease where the rent included one plough's work yearly and two autumn boons, as other tenants in Walton do yearly; there is a reference to hedges and ditches (but none to stone walls) and a house let was repaired initially by the landlord, the tenant to maintain it subsequently, except where large timbers were needed for repair work. Walton also had its two corn mills, located on Walton Hall land and powered by the stream, dammed to make the lake in which Walton Hall still stands on its island, as it stood in medieval times as a fortified house.

Some indication of the way in which land was held in medieval Walton derives from the undated Wytbelt and King family marriage settlement of c1300, which lists the then Wytbelt properties of William Wytbelt of Walton which were to pass to Richard King of Crofton on his marriage to Wytbelt's daughter Isabel, which were:

> 1 house and croft in Walton
> 6 acres in Walton
> 7 half acres dispersed in Walton
> 1.5 perches in the Moors in Walton

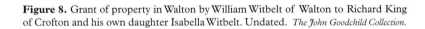

Figure 8. Grant of property in Walton by William Witbelt of Walton to Richard King of Crofton and his own daughter Isabella Witbelt. Undated. *The John Goodchild Collection.*

11 perches dispersed in the Moors in Walton
2 half perches dispersed in the Moors in Walton
2 quarter perches dispersed in the Moors in Walton

subject to the payment of 6d per annum in silver payable to the grantor (Figure 8).

Places and People

In the years 1251 to 1252 there were court proceedings between Walton and Chevet as to their respective rights over the common land which lay between them; Walton Common is still a recognisable place in our own day. Significantly the dispute was both carried through the courts in the names of the freeholders, great and small, of the two townships, and it was carried to the highest courts of England, no doubt at considerable expense. Reference is made in the surviving case documents to one Adam de Wytbelt of Walton,

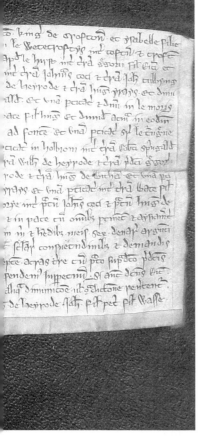

although the non-local court clerk misspelt his name; his descendants were to live in Walton until the time of the Black Death, but something of their story can be recovered from surviving papers, and it is an interesting one. The Adam of the 1251-52 lawsuit had a son, William, and two daughters are known of; one daughter married a Robert son of William de Heghrode, another family of Walton small freeholders who are mentioned again below, and the other daughter was named Margaret. Margaret had a daughter Alice, who is referred to in the deeds by name as Alice daughter of Margaret Wytbelt: this is not a unique type of naming in Walton at about this time, and it may suggest illegitimacy. The son was William Wytbelt. The name, apparently derived from a white belt, ie a nickname, William Whitbelt confirmed to the Hospitallers – knights of St John of Jerusalem – the land given to them by Thomas Tyrell, perhaps his father-in-law, by a deed of the later 1200s and his name first appears in the surviving Wakefield Manor Court Rolls, which begin in 1274, in 1275, so he was obviously a tenant of Wakefield Manor, presumably holding land outside Walton to so qualify him. The 1297 taxation return returns his taxation on one ox, one cow, two quarters of oats, half a quarter of wheat, when he was one of only six men taxed in Walton; his tax bill totalled thirteen shillings, while the largest sum taxed was 21s 8d.

There are many references to the name William Wytbelt in deeds between 1303 and 1335 as grantor, grantee or witness; given the long time span between a first reference in 1275 to one of 1335, possibly there were two men of that name. In 1324 William Wytbelt was acting as an official of the Wakefield manor court, in 1316 he was sued there for sixteen and a half quarters of rye – a large quantity of corn, bought but not paid for – and he was ordered to make satisfaction, and in 1328 fined for not attending the court.

But William Wytbelt's spinster niece, Alice daughter of Margaret, seems to have been a woman who kept the village tongues wagging. She sued in court for debts which she claimed were due to her; blood was drawn from her in 1317 – ie she had been physically attacked. She sued for wages claimed to be due from John Cokewald in 1317 too: these were for a period bewteen Whitsuntide and Martinmas in 1310, some seven years earlier; her claim was found to be vexatious, as others of her law actions may have been, and she was fined 6d for having made it. She was also concerned as a landowner with the transfer of land. Another Alice, daughter of a younger Adam Wytbelt and his wife Beatrice, both of Walton, married in 1348 when her mother was a widow; her first husband was Roger Scot and her second John Storr, a man who lived in Walton but owned a moiety of the Manor of Shelley – obviously a man of means and station.

There were probably three male Wytbelts in the next generation: Adam and Henry who seem to have died without male heirs, and William too, whose daughter Isabel was his heiress. Isabel's father had both inherited and himself acquired land, and upon his daughter's marriage the estate was settled upon her new husband, Richard King of Crofton and upon her too, by deed. This fascinating deed survives, as a kind of middle-class marriage settlement of a very early and most rare kind, so far at least as survival is concerned; it has no date and its seal has gone; it possibly dates from the very late thirteenth century.

Isabel Wytbelt was the heiress and her husband was Richard King of Crofton: the origin of his name is uncertain, but his father was one Adam King. The pair lived at Walton, which had and has a common boundary with Crofton, and in 1297 he was taxed on a horse, two cows, ten sheep, three quarters of oats and three of wheat: he was very nearly the richest man in Walton. He not only acquired land through his marriage with Isabel Wytbelt, but purchased more, while he also tenanted some too. As he had a son grown up by the date of a deed of 1310, perhaps Isabel Wytbelt was his second wife; unlike the Wytbelts there are no references to Richard King in the Wakefield Court Rolls until 1316, possibly when he came into the Wytbelt property held of that manor. By Isabel, Richard King had a son who, like his probably earlier son, who became a priest, was also called John. This latter and younger son John may have been he who was described in the Poll Tax return of 1379, when presumably he was an elderly man of about sixty, as a smith.

Two places of the name of Walton are listed in the Wapentake of Agbrigg in the 1379 Poll Tax lists: both have apparently recognisable Walton near Wakefield surnames in them, and they may correlate to the Walton near Wakefield and the part of that township which was separated from that village and lay dispersed in parts of West Bretton village: the township of West Bretton was also largely in Sandal Magna parish.

The 1379 Walton Poll Tax listing shows twenty-four persons, householders, paying at the normal 4d a head of the middle class in society; in Sandal, all thirty-two also paid at 4d, while at Chevet, eleven paid at 4d and Sir John Bosvile at 20s, the sum also paid from Bretton Hall. No reference is made to Walton Hall at all.

Achilles Bosvile of Chevet was son of Sir John, a knight, whose own mother Alice had brought the Monk family interest in Chevet to the Bosviles upon her marriage to a younger son of that family, then of Darfield. Sir John was alive in 1382 and his son Achilles had a chaplain in 1407 and was described as an esquire, buying land in Chevet between 1393 and the mid 1420s. He may have married a daughter of John King and thereby brought that family's Chevet property to the Bosviles; he certainly died without issue, and was succeeded by his brother John who had inherited his mother's Newark estate at Stoke, but then moved to Chevet, where he was ancestor of succeeding owners of Chevet to 1753. A significant point about Achilles Bosvile may be his forename, which presumably suggests his father's knowledge of classical Greek literature, or at least Homer's tales, by the 1370s.

Returning to the King family, John King the blacksmith, whose wife was Agnes, seems to have died between 1379 and 1391, but to have had a son John, described in deeds as John son of John King of Walton, and another son Adam who was of (ancestral) Crofton. The King line appears to have terminated with another priest, John son of John son of John, who was alive in 1399-1400, and he serves to introduce such aspects as can be recovered of the obvious interest taken by the sturdy middle class of Walton, Sandal and Chevet in religion – an interest shown in very practical terms by their willingness to spend money upon certain ecclesiastical institutions. No monastic house at all seems to have owned land at Walton, other than that given by the enthusiastic Walton men to the Hospitallers, but one Walton man seems to have been responsible for the establishment of a chapel in Walton, that John de Walton whose father was the Richard King who ultimately married Isabel Wytbelt. Master John de Walton is described in 1310 as son of Richard King, and again in 1323 and 1329, and also as John King of Walton, chaplain. In 1314 he was chaplain of a church at Walton and still apparently by 1333 he was rector of a church of his own. John de Walton, chaplain, and William de Walton, clerk (in holy orders) were both witnesses to a deed of 1369-70; a John de Walton, chaplain, acquired land which had belonged to John King of Walton, also a chaplain, in 1399-1400 and was dead by 1414; Adam de Walton, rector of a mediety of Rillington Church in the East Riding, owned land at Walton which had come from his dead mother and his sister, and it may be that successive generations of the King family produced sons who became priests – perhaps younger sons. In the obvious absence of parish registers, and at this time of any wills made by these people, family relationships are often impossible to trace. By custom within the Archbishopric of York, on death a man's property went to the eldest son and one third of his goods to his widow; a will was a costly non-necessity.

There was also a recognisable group of Walton men – and women – who appear in the surviving deeds, not as parties buying or selling, nor as grantors or grantees, and never as witnesses, but who are described solely as the owners of properties adjoining those which were particularised as sold (etc) by a specific deed. They cannot be copyholders, as neither Wakefield nor Walton manors seem to have possessed copyhold in Walton: they were presumably yet smaller freeholders. They appear in the earlier, undated, deeds and in dated ones up to and including 1312, but not beyond that date. Their names:

Adam son of John	Peter son of Rate	John son of Peter
Malie wife of Wm	Christiania dau of Alan	Peter son of Henry
Rate son of Hugh *	John son of Malle	Thomas son of Walta
Thomas son of Hugh	Hugh Grays	Wm Malpas
Alice Exlet	Wm de Heyer	

* a strip owner in November 1317

The form of these names – as Adam son of John – also disappears locally during the fourteenth century, and by the time of the Poll Tax of 1379, only Beatrix wife of Henry son of John, a widow, remained to be described in this manner.

The Shaw family's fortunes can be followed through medieval times too. No Shaw was of Walton in the Poll Tax list of 1379, nor is any Shaw mentioned in the Wakefield manor court rolls of an earlier period, although a Shaw family did exist within the manor of Wakefield at Sowerby and Halifax. The name appears locally as variously de Shaw, del Shaw, and as Shagh, Schagh, Schae, Scagh, essentially always Shaw, a name indicating a wood. But in 1389 Richard de Scagh (of an earlier Ossett family) bought a house and land in Walton, presumably as a relative newcomer, and land in Sandal, while the same man, now living in Walton, bought a house and a substantial sixteen acres of land in Sandal in 1394, and in

1396-97 he bought a further house and land in Middle Walton. He was of Walton when a party to a deed, along with two chaplains, in 1399, and he then probably moved as another deed of 1399 refers to him as of Sandal. He had a wife Joan and references occur to him down to 1415 when he gave land for a chantry chapel's endowment in Sandal church to the vicar and two chaplains there, the land lying widely placed in Sandal, Walton and Newbiggin (ie Newmillerdam).

A Roger de Shaw also appears in a deed of 1400 as of Walton, and again in 1407-08; his relationship to Richard Shaw is unknown, and none of these people left wills. Richard Shaw of Sandal left two sons. The genealogy is unclear, and in any case quite insignificant, except to remark that the properties obviously passed, in Shaw hands and through several generations, to a John Shaw who was admitted to his father Richard's copyhold Hospitallers' estates in Walton in 1524, paying twelve pence relief. He moved to Seacroft near Leeds and made his will in 1526, his son John Shaw junior being admitted to the Walton property in 1527, to which his brother, also of Seacroft, was admitted in 1538. In 1542 the brother, William, a major taxpayer in Seacroft in 1546, sold all his Sandal, Walton and Pledwick estate to Christopher Field, a Wakefield mercer who died in 1557, for £15. It passed from him to Matthew Field who was a merchant in London and from him by sale to the Chevet Hall estate. A further John Shaw, a tenant in Sandal and of that village, made his will in 1556 and died in 1558; the relationship is again unknown.

It was apparently the first Richard Shaw who was the most major land acquirer of his family: for probably a period of thirty-eight years up to at least 1426 he bought land at Shooter's Hill on the outskirts of Wakefield but in Sandal township, and in Sandal, in Milnthorpe and in Newbiggin as well as properties at Walton and at Kettlethorpe, a hamlet in Crigglestone township but adjoining the Sandal boundary. In 1409 he was one of number of local men buying tithes from St Stephen's College, Westminster, and the Shaws were benefactors to mother church; a number of ecclesiastics, incumbents and chaplains were parties to Shaw deeds of 1415 and 1490-91.

The three townships
The place name Sandal means a sandy nook of land. As we have seen, Sandal was a township with a number of dispersed settlements – Sandal Magna, Milnthorpe etc – but it had a system of open strip fields, apparently four in number, which served the whole of the hamlets. These were the Old Field, the Castle Field, the Pucknall Field and the South Field; there were also the water meadows of

Sandal Ings, and the commons – the South Moors and Sandal Moor. Many medieval field names are known, together with the names of shutts, or groups of strips, in the fields. Walton, on the other hand, was a township with a nucleated centre – the part now known as Walton itself – with handsful of cottages at Upper and Lower Walton and the lost village of Woodhouse. The place name Walton means the hamlet of the Welsh or old men, suggesting settlement at an early date, perhaps in the sixth or seventh centuries, and it may be significant that at the time of the Domesday survey of 1086 Walton had an unusually large area of cultivated land. Both Sandal and Walton townships were part of Sandal ecclesiastical parish. Chevet, whose name means simply the ridge, lay in Royston parish and apparently consisted of a single nucleated hamlet whose freeholds were inherited or bought out by the owners of the later Chevet Hall estate, and the village was entirely removed by the early sixteenth century: in 1517 it was reported that the place was deserted. Walton again had its own field system, consisting of the North, South and Great Fields, with the Long Moor, the Great Meadow, the Ings and Thorn Green. In Walton reference is made to the medieval bridges over the system of slight streams which intersect the township, and to various wells – the Great, Little and Lower Hazle wells.

The local economy was essentially an agricultural one, with arable farming and animal husbandry conjoined: shepherds are mentioned and there are lists of animals in the 1297 taxation returns. Medieval references occur to the occupations of smith, roper, shepherd, carpenter, indicating the usual service trades of a rural community, but perhaps in the case of ropemaking an envisaged wider market. Place names suggest areas of woodland, and a number of hunting parks, especially Sandal Park, which was associated with Sandal Castle; it is less certain that Haw Park and Hare Park were also such. Coal may have been mined in Walton, where it outcrops and where by the seventeenth century at least there were substantial workings; coal also outcrops in Crigglestone township, which adjoins upon Sandal. No references occur to the working of the massive beds of sandstone at Walton or Newmillerdam, but as all the hamlets concerned, with the possible exception of Chevet, were stone-built rather than of timber from at least the sixteenth century, it seems likely that some more than minor use was made of this natural resource.

Extensive spiritual provision was made for the townships of Sandal, Chevet and Walton in medieval times. In the case of Sandal – the head of an ecclesiastical parish which embraced Sandal itself,

Walton cum (West) Bretton and Crigglestone townships – a church existed probably in the 1090s, although it is by no means certain that the Domesday reference of 1086 is to a church there. Chevet, as we have seen, was in the parish of Royston, another widespread ecclesiastical parish, and by the beginning of the fourteenth century chapels of ease, to enable local parishioners to more easily enjoy spiritual benefits, existed at both Chevet and Woolley, in Royston parish. At Woolley the (largely later rebuilt) medieval church survives, and contains a tympanum or doorhead of Norman type, dated by its style to no later than the mid 1100s, and the church is mentioned in documents from c1258. A number of such chapels of ease existed in Royston parish, and in regard to that at Chevet by 1207; in the year 1300 it was specified that the vicar of Royston was not to do any ecclesiastical service in the chapel of Chevet. This chapel was apparently provided at the cost of the inhabitants there, rather than of any great landowner, and such was also the case with the chapel at Walton. The Chevet church stood outside the village of Chevet: the first documentary reference to it is of 1286, and a deed of 1322 refers to land between the village and the chapel, and one of 1348 to two strips (selions) adjoining the ditches of the chapel. An earlier but undated deed refers to land lying in the Kirkfield of Chevet. The location of the Chevet church is not known: the tithe award map of c1840 shows the Chapel Close near to the suggested site of Chevet village, to the west of Chevet Hall, but the Pilkington estate settlement deed of 1879 and its map show the Upper, Near and Low Chapel Closes below Chevet Farm, half a mile south of the Hall (Figure 9). The chapel at Chevet, like those at Walton and elsewhere, seems to have been served by chaplains who are variously described as such or with the title 'Sir'; possibly the differentiation was as between those who were merely in deacon's orders and those who were fully priested. Certainly considerable numbers of them are mentioned in the hundreds of surviving deeds. The Chevet church, like that at Walton, was comparatively short lived, and the last reference to it is in 1339; perhaps the reference to its ditches in 1348 is to its ruins. A deed of 1641 refers to the Sheep Close alias Chapel Close, but the name of the chapel as associated with field names, lingered on into Victorian times. In the adjoining parish of Sandal Magna, the townships of Walton and Crigglestone each had their own chapel of ease. The latter, at Chapelthorpe, survived until the Reformation, until 1547, and was later re-opened and survives, in much later buildings, today; it is first mentioned in connection with an assault there in 1314. The chapel of ease at Walton existed by

Figure 9. 1850 Ordnance Survey map used as an estate map showing the Pilkington estates in the Wakefield area in 1879. The Chapel Closes are shown as numbers 18, 19 and 33. *The John Goodchild Collection.*

1312, and just may have been the foundation made by a local priest and small landowner at Walton, John King, chaplain, apparently otherwise known as John de Walton, chaplain. In 1330 Henry de Walton, chaplain, had a grant confirmed in Wakefield Manor Court

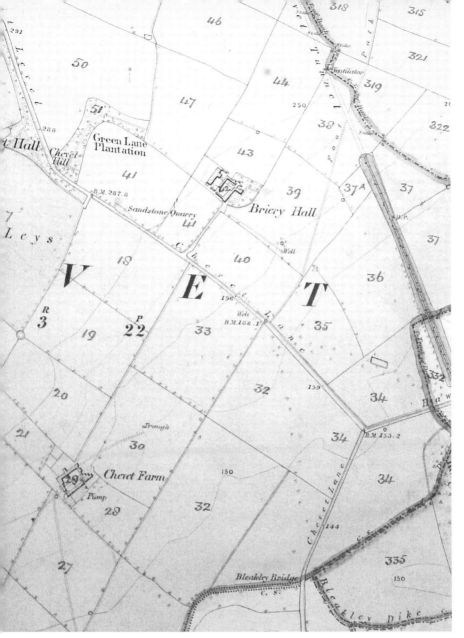

of land as an augmentation of his salary as chantry priest in Sandal, and in 1339 the Rector of Sandal church paid 6s 8d (33p) tax on his profits from Walton church while by 1343 Adam de Walton, Rector of , as variety of the living of, Rillington near Malton, was heir to his mother and his brother John – possibly the earlier John de Walton. There appears to be some evidence of descent of property to sons of these clergymen, and of a clerical family in successive generations at

Walton; there was apparently no ecclesiastical objection to marriage of a deacon within the church. Other gifts of land in Walton were to earlier priests working the mother living of Sandal.

One might have anticipated that something of the formal dedication of these chapels might have been recorded in the archiepiscopal records at York, but such is not the case. Indeed the Director of the Borthwick Institute at York, where such records are now found, suggests in a letter to the writer of 1991 that,

> *Often, I suspect, licensings and consecrations of buildings were not recorded in the registers with any regularity.*

The last reference to the chapel at Walton appears to be one of 1348.

The disappearance of the chapels at both Walton and Chevet may perhaps be linked with the advent of the Black Death's great surge across England in the mid-fourteenth century; so too, perhaps, may be the disappearance of the Walton village of Woodhouse or Woodsome.

One unusual – though by no means unique – feature of the story of both Walton and Chevet is that these deeds demonstrate (in regard to Chevet) and from another source in regard to Walton, that estates there passed in one family, by marriage (and of course added to by purchases) from probably pre-Conquest times into modern times. The Chevet estate, originally in part but later in whole, was sold in 1753 but then only to another member of the owning family, and survived as a whole until 1951; the Walton estate of the Watertons similarly survived until sold by Edmund Waterton (and his creditors) to Edward Simpson the soapboiler in 1877 – in each instance they had passed (in part) through families connected by marriage for the best part of one thousand years.

It is fortunate that such large collections of the deeds and papers of the latterday Pilkington family should have survived, which, used here with other source materials, give so detailed a picture of the names, the families, sometimes the personal peculiarities, of some members of these medieval communities, along with some detail of their homes, their occupations, their religious concerns, their neighbours, and of the very topography and appearance of their communities, and how, when and even why they changed.

Sources

Material in the John Goodchild collection, below Drury Lane Library, Wakefield.

10. YOUNG WOMEN AT WORK IN OSSETT IN 1851

by Deborah Scriven

IN 1851 ABOUT A QUARTER OF the female population of England and Wales was in waged work. These women, who made up about thirty per cent of the entire labour force, were mainly employed in four activities: domestic service, textile and clothing industries and in agriculture.

In particular, women were engaged in domestic service, and by the end of the nineteenth century it was the largest single occupation in the United Kingdom, for either men or women. There were, however, considerable regional variations in the numbers of women employed as servants. London, for example, was the great centre for servant employment, while in provincial areas it varied according to the character of the local economy.

This was true of Yorkshire, where, in the rural East and North Ridings, over half of all working women were employed as servants, while in the more industrialised West Riding, servants were outnumbered by women at work in the textile and clothing trades. Even within the West Riding there were differences. It has been estimated that in Wakefield about twenty-five per cent of young women aged fifteen to nineteen years were employed as domestic servants in 1851, while in the neighbouring industrial district of Dewsbury, only 9.8 per cent of girls were thus employed.

It is possible to survey women's occupations using information provided by the Census. This information must, however, be interpreted with caution. Women's work, particularly that of married women, often went unrecorded, because it was casual or part-time work. However the occupations of young single women were usually more accurately recorded, though inconsistencies in the terms used could cause problems in interpretation. Domestic service was described in several ways, using terms such as 'household duties' and 'housekeeper' as well as 'general servant', making it difficult to distinguish between those with paid work and those working in their own home.

As Ossett was a township in the Dewsbury district it is possible to survey the occupations of the young women of the town to see if the estimate of 9.8 per cent employment in domestic service was, in fact, accurate. In 1851, Ossett was a large, straggling township with a population of 6,265. Although there was some coal mining and a number of farms, it was predominantly a textile town of small-scale enterprises, specialising in the use of reclaimed wool in woollen manufacture.

According to the 1851 Census there were 346 young women aged fifteen to nineteen years in the town. Four cannot be identified and seven were only visitors, so 335 are left to be surveyed as to their occupations. The vast majority were single though, surprisingly, nineteen were married, a higher proportion than expected, given that the average age at marriage for women at that time was twenty-three years. Of these women, 271 or eighty per cent were listed as employed, forty-four in some form of domestic service.

Seven were daughters doing domestic work in their own households. Martha Peace aged seventeen years was described as a 'housekeeper', and looked after her widowed father, a stonemason, and six brothers and sisters aged five to fourteen years. David Riley, a handloom weaver was also widowed, so his daughter Martha took on the domestic role of her dead mother and kept house for her father, four brothers and sisters under fourteen years and two older sisters, Sarah, a rag sorter and Susannah, a cloth burler.

Most of the thirty-six wage-earning servants lived in single-servant households and were employed by some of the emerging middle class inhabitants of Ossett. Sarah Hewitt worked for Sarah Illingworth, a widow, who had six children aged five to nineteen years. She was a cloth manufacturer who employed nine men. Thomas Mitchell of Dale Street employed Hannah Horton to look after a household that consisted of himself, his wife, Sarah, and three sons, aged six months, two and five years. Mitchell was also a cloth manufacturer, a well-known and respected Weslyan and a Liberal. He was later described in his obituary in the *Ossett Observer* as 'a most vigorous, animated and fluent speaker'. Joseph and Joshua Wilby were cloth manufacturers employing twenty-five men in a weaving shop and dryhouse at Low Common. They were both unmarried and employed Eliza Hemingway as a servant in a household which also included three adult sisters.

The Greaves brothers and their father had extensive business interests in Ossett, owning a mill in Gawthorpe, warehouses, workshops, a counting house, and cottages. Two of them employed servants. Jane Fletcher worked for Thomas Greaves, a retired blanket manufacturer, and his wife, Mary, while Joshua employed Mary Ann

Figure 1. South Ossett Church.

Sheard to look after himself and his daughter, Jane.

Some households employed more than one servant. As might be expected of a man who had a position to keep up, the Reverend Denis Neary, vicar of South Ossett, employed both Ann Hawksworth, aged fifteen years and Ann Roberts, aged thirty years as general servants. Neary was the son of a farmer in Northern Ireland and had come to Ossett as curate to the vicar of Holy Trinity. In 1850 he was appointed to the new parish of South Ossett. As a man of 'remarkable zeal and energy' he was the driving force behind the building of the new parish church which was erected in 1851 (Figure 1). His fellow clergyman, the Reverend Oliver Collins, the curate of Ossett at Holy Trinity church in the marketplace, employed both Sarah Richards and Emma Huntsman in his household. Collins was a man well respected by ministers of other denominations, his life and character being considered as exemplary.

William Wood Wiseman, a doctor, another prominent citizen of the town, was much involved in the railway mania of the 1840s, as a director of the Wakefield and Dewsbury atmospheric railway. He lived in Springstone House on Streetside and had a large household containing his wife, four daughters and two sons, his sister, a governess, his male pupil, aged sixteen years, an errand boy and Sarah Baines, aged nineteen years, the general servant (Figures 2 and 3).

Joseph Whitaker, an unmarried master maltster, lived in Town End with a young nephew. He employed his cousin Susannah as housekeeper and kept two other female servants, including Eliza Hartley. He had inherited his business from an uncle, Joseph Ingham, and took an active part in public affairs for many years.

Another two-servant household was that of the widower Joseph Rowley, a worsted and woollen manufacturer. Emma Oldroyd and

Parish or Township of Gawthorpe | Ecclesiastical District of | City or Borough of | Town of | Village of

Name of Street, Place, or Road, and Name or No. of House	Name and Surname of each Person who abode in the house, on the Night of the 30th March, 1851	Relation to Head of Family	Condition	Age of Males	Age of Females	Rank, Profession, or Occupation	Where Born	Whether Blind, or Deaf-and-Dumb
Town Knowl	Francis Heaton	Head	Mar	55		Journeyman Carpenter	Yorks Ossett	
	Amelia do	Wife	Mar		44	Cloth Burler	Yorks do	
	Richard do	Son	U	20		Woolsier at Mill	do do	
	Frank do	Son	U	16		Piecer at Mill (Woollen)	do do	
	Elizabeth do	Daur	U		12	at Home	do do	
	Alfred do	do	U	7		Scholar	do do	
	Ann do	Mother	Wid		85		do do	
Town Knowl	William Wood Wiseman	Head	Mar	44		London Genl. Practitioner M.R.C.S. England & L.S.A.	do Sandal magna	
	Mary do	Wife	Mar		32	Wife	do Soothill	
	Elizabeth do	Daur	U		12	Scholar at Home	do Ossett	
	Mary Agnes do	Daur	U		9	do	do do	
	Matilda Jane do	Daur	U		7	do	do do	
	John Greaves do	Son	U	5		do	do do	
	William Henry do	Son	U	3		do	do do	
	Emily Gertrude do	Daur	U		1	do	do do	
	Hannah do	Sister	U		30	Lady	do Sandal magna	
	Sophia Whitworth	Governess	U		23	Teaching	do Wakefield	
	John Dixon	Pupil	U	16		Student	do Wragby	
	Sarah Baines	Servant	U		19	House Servant	do Horbury	
	Edward Blackburn	Servant	U	14		Errand Boy	do Thornhill	
12 U B			Total of Persons	10	10			

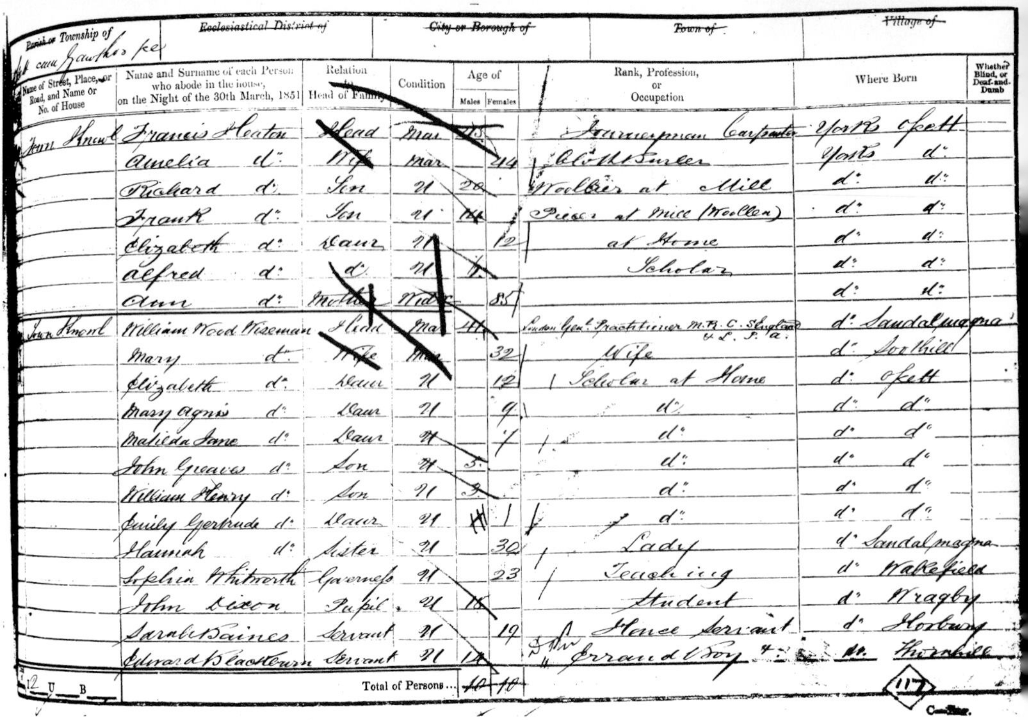

Figure 2. The 1851 census entry for the Wiseman family of Springstone House. *By permission of the Public Record Office.*

Sarah Thomas worked for Rowley and his son Edwin in the house near their mill on Owl Lane, Gawthorpe. Like Wiseman, Rowley was caught up in railway mania being a director of the Midland, Barnsley, Sheffield, Dewsbury, Leeds and Bradford Railway. The woollen and worsted business prospered and by 1871 he employed 107 hands. Edwin eventually carried on from his father and died a wealthy man with a large estate near Penrith.

However not all householders who employed servants could be regarded as middle class. Others were artisans or tradespeople. John Helliwell was a wheelwright and victualler who employed Ann Appleby to work in a large household containing his wife and brother, also a wheelwright, and four children. Rebecca Lister, on the other hand, may have had an easier life as she had only Thomas Mitchell, a tinner and ironmonger, and his wife to look after.

Figure 3. Springstone House in 2001. *Kate Taylor.*

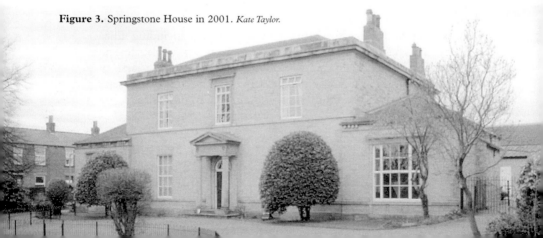

Charlotte Kidson worked for the grocer, George Pickard, perhaps to free his wife from domestic duties so that she could help him in the shop. Elizabeth Ainsworth, a widow, also had a shop and employed Mary Ann Dews to do the domestic chores.

Employment as a domestic servant was not popular among Ossett-born women. Although one-third of servants did come from Ossett itself, more were recruited from the surrounding villages such as Horbury, Earlsheaton and Thornhill. Others were born further afield, in Sheffield, Snaith and Sherburn. All however were born within the county of Yorkshire, except for two from North Wales. Ellen Parry was from Beaumaris and worked for Nancy Oakes, a proprietor of house and land who also employed a male farm servant from Ireland. Susannah Oates was born in Barmouth and was employed by James Illingworth, the keeper of the *Hammer and Anvil* inn on Streetside (Figure 4).

So there were few young women engaged in domestic service in Ossett in 1851, and the estimate of 9.8 per cent is substantially accurate. None of them was described as a farm servant, so it would appear that agriculture, one of the big four areas of employment nationally, did not employ large numbers in the town.

Of the remainder of young Ossett women, two worked in schools. Ruth Nettleton was described as a pupil teacher while Sarah Webster was a school assistant. They could have taught at one of the ten private academies, National and Infant schools and Wesleyan day and Sunday schools or at the free school which had been founded in the mid-eighteenth century, by subscription. In 1851 the headmaster was William Cullingworth and his wife Marianne was a schoolmistress. In later years Cullingworth's younger daughter, Matilda, also joined the profession and kept a school off Dale Street.

Women virtually monopolised the clothing trades in the nineteenth century and eight young Ossett women were described as seamstresses or dressmakers. It is possible that they were employed as outworkers by milliners. These were not just hat makers, but

Figure 4. The *Hammer and Stithy* in 2001, formerly the *Hammer and Anvil*.

highly skilled women with practical abilities and expert knowledge of dress and fashion.

However the great majority of young women in Ossett were employed in the textile industries. In 1851 the textile industries of the West Riding employed a total of 27,765 females, of whom 13,345 were under twenty years of age. In Ossett 215 out of a total of 335 women aged fifteen to nineteen years, including six of the married women, were employed in textile work.

The manufacturers of Ossett were particularly involved in the mungo and shoddy trades. These involved mixing reclaimed wool with virgin sheep's wool to produce cloth which was cheaper and aimed at the mass market. Soft rags such as stocking and flannels were ground to make shoddy while hard or cloth rags became mungo. Rag pickers or sorters were employed by rag dealers to sort the rags. Many rag warehouses were small-scale enterprises, few employing more than ten women. The work was unhealthy, because of dust, and asthma was a common complaint. Ossett had a reputation particularly for the production of mungo which was used both in the local mills and in other parts of the Clothing District. The local woollen manufacturers produced good quality cloths such as beavers, witneys and meltons.

Although the textile industries employed both men and women, the latter were segregated into the low paid processes. Women were employed mainly as rag sorters, cloth burlers, who picked out knots and other imperfections in the cloth after it had returned from the fulling, and warpers, who formed warps into webs for the loom. In Ossett seventy-seven of the young women were employed as rag sorters and sixty-three as cloth burlers.

Samuel Jubb in his history of the shoddy trade in Batley (1860) clearly shows the wage differentials between men and women. Female rag sorters received 6s 6d (32.5p) to 7s (35p) per week, while their male foremen received 20s (£1) to 25s (£1 25p). Male rag grinders received 16s (80p) to 26s (£1 30p) while female burlers got the same as rag sorters. Female warpers were slightly better paid at 8s (40p) per week.

Jubb states that wages in Ossett were slightly lower than those in Batley. In 1853 the *Wakefield Express* reported that rag pickers in Ossett went on strike in an effort to advance their wages from one penny to one penny farthing per hour. The newspaper reported their work as 'dirty disagreable employment' and that the women were 'well worthy of the renumeration they solicit'. However, the Ossett rag masters brought in Irish workers who were prepared to work for lower wages, while many of the Ossett rag pickers found work in Dewsbury and Batley, where they were able to earn more.

Surprisingly, nearly twenty per cent of young women in Ossett had no stated occupation according to the 1851 Census. There may have been a number of reasons for this. They may have been genuinely seeking paid work but were unemployed at that time. Research has shown that, nationally, around forty per cent of girls aged fifteen to nineteen years were unoccupied. The figure was much lower for counties such as the West Riding where work in the textile industries was plentiful. It is therefore unlikely that many young women in Ossett were genuinely unemployed. On the other hand, they may actually have had waged work but because a 'proper' job tended to be seen in terms of the male breadwinner, their work was not recorded. Most likely, the majority of these young women were in the hidden economy ie. engaged in work in the home.

In the Victorian era, the ideology of 'separate spheres' became common, whereby married women were expected to stay at home to care for husband and children while the husband went out to work to support his family. Only young, single women were expected to be part of the workforce. However the reality was very different as wives too often had to work because the husband's income on its own was insufficient. Many took work into the home such as childminding or washing, though this was never recorded in the Census. Mary Scott of Ossett who had a year-old son made extra income by taking in a lodger. Mary and Thomas Whitworth and their seven month old son perhaps could not yet afford to set up a separate household and so lived with Mary's parents and her four brothers and sisters.

Some of the young, single women of Ossett may have remained at home because their fathers were sufficiently wealthy to keep them in idleness and employed servants to do the domestic work. Mark Stephenson had a daughter, Bridget, who was of an age to assist her mother, but in fact he employed Mary Beaumont from Cudworth to do domestic work. Stephenson was quite a large employer in the town, having both farming and cloth manufacturing interests.

John Briggs, and George Wilby were woollen cloth manufacturers of some stature, Briggs employing eleven men. Emma Wilby and her two adult sisters were described in the Census as 'manufacturer's daughters' while their brother Charles Henry was a 'manufacturer's son'. Charles later gave up woollen manufacturing to go to Canada, where he remained for nearly thirty years as a marine store dealer. None of John Briggs' three daughters worked outside the home though his son, aged sixteen years was a woollen cloth weaver. The plumber and glazier, Joseph Mitchell was able to support his widowed mother and three adult sisters, so none of them had to go out to work to supplement the family income.

Other young women may have been kept at home to help with the family business. Ellen Walker's father, John was keeper of the *Flying Horse* pub on Streetside while Sarah Giggal may have had to help her father, Robert in his shop (Figure 5).

The majority of young women without occupations were probably kept at home to help their mothers with housework and caring for siblings, domestic servants in all but name. Yet it is likely that the service they provided at home was far more valuable to the household than any wages they could earn outside the house. Rebecca Wilby was the only daughter in a household with six brothers aged four to twenty-one years. All of them worked, except the youngest. Joshua Butterworth and his wife had five daughters and a year old son, so that it is likely that Mary as the eldest was expected to help her mother. Nathaniel Giggal, a woollen cloth weaver also had a large household, comprising four adult sons who were all woollen cloth weavers, two daughters aged ten and twelve who were rag sorters, a younger daughter aged seven and Susanna aged fifteen years.

Martha Harrap's father, John, was a woollen manufacturer of some substance who employed sixteen men, and might have been expected to employ a house servant. However it would seem that it was Martha, the only girl, who was expected to help her mother care for the family, which included six brothers, two described as 'manufacturers sons', two were woollen cloth weavers and the two youngest, at ten and fourteen years old, were scholars.

The Speight household was similar. Emma, aged fifteen years, was described in the Census as 'scholar' and therefore spared domestic duties, but her eighteen year old sister, Mary was described as 'house

Figure 5. The *Flying Horse* in 2001. *Kate Taylor.*

servant'. It was unlikely that she worked for another household, so, like Martha Harrap, Mary was probably kept at home to help her mother who had twelve children altogether, eleven surviving into adulthood. Their father, John Speight was a rag dealer and an industrial pioneer, being one of the first mungo makers at his premises at Northfield Mill, Church Street. His wife, Hannah, took an active interest in the business and, unusually for a women, was accorded an obituary in the *Ossett Observer* on her death in 1887.

There were other households where one adult daughter was kept at home, but her sisters went out to work. Ann Laycock's older sister Elizabeth was employed as a cloth burler, while Eliza Stocks had two older sisters who were both described as housemaids. Yet it is impossible to determine from the information given in the Census whether Ann and Eliza had been specially chosen to be the daughter kept at home to help mother or whether they were perhaps at home with a disability which precluded waged work.

The Census provides a useful snapshot of the employment situation of young women in Ossett. It shows that while there were many textile businesses in the town offering employment, the market for domestic servants was not large. On the other hand, many of the young women at home, ostensibly without occupation, were probably involved in domestic work in their own households.

Notes and References

Primary Sources
Census enumerators books for Ossett-cum-Gawthorpe. 1851 PRO: HO 107/2325.
White, W – *Directory and gazeteer of Leeds, Bradford …and the whole of the clothing districts.* 1853 (reprinted David and Charles).
The *Wakefield Express*, 1853.
Jubb, S *The history of the shoddy trade,* London, Houlston and Wright, 1860.
Baines, E *The woollen manufacture of England* (reprinted David and Charles), 1858.

Secondary Sources
Bythell, D 'Women in the workforce' in O'Brien, P K and Quinault, R. (eds) *The industrial revolution and British society.* Cambridge. Cambridge University Press. P.31-53, 1993.
Golby, J (ed) *Community and families* Cambridge, Cambridge University Press in association with the Open University, 1997.
Higgs, E 'Domestic service and household production' in John, A (ed) *Unequal opportunities: women's employment in England 1800-1918.* Oxford, Blackwell p.125-52, 1986.
Higgs, E *A clearer sense of the Census* London, HMSO, 1996.
Jordan, E 'Female unemployment in England and Wales 1851-1911: an examination of the census figures for fifteen to nineteen year olds' *Social History* 13, p.175-190, 1998.
Smith, B Index to the 1851 census for Ossett-cum-Gawthorpe (database), 1994

Acknowledgements

I would like to thank Brian Smith and David Scriven for making their own research available to me.

11. BREWING IN WAKEFIELD: SOME HISTORICAL NOTES

by John Goodchild

THE BREWING OF BEER is referred to in documents dating from as early as about 6,000 BC; beer was then being made in Babylonia as it was later in ancient Egypt, China, Rome and so forth. It was probably known in Iron Age Britain and numerous references to the appointment of aletasters and the brewing of beer which was not up to the necessary quality occur in the medieval court rolls of the great Manor of Wakefield, while by the seventeenth century the major local authority, the West Riding magistrates, were licensing individual inns which were brewing their own beers.

Until the eighteenth century, most beer was made in inn brewhouses, in ordinary houses, and in the brewhouses of larger country houses – and some cellar books of those country houses survive in the John Goodchild Collection. In London, however, the common brewer – he who brewed for sale to public houses and for general sale – became of significance during the eighteenth century and the trade of the common brewer soon spread into the English provinces, a common brewer being at work in Leeds during the 1750s.

Until the 1830s most of the Wakefield and district innkeepers brewed their own beer in brewhouses forming part of their own premises, using water from those wells on their premises which are a constant feature of contemporary advertisements for the sale of inns, and using malt produced by local maltsters. The earliest common brewer in Wakefield on a commercial scale appears to have been Robert Harrison, who is referred to as the only brewer in Wakefield at the period of the first detailed trade directory, published in 1781, although he had occupied property in Kirkgate in Wakefield for at least twenty years previously. Harrison had taken his son, Robert, into partnership by 1784 and he was later able to live in retirement, describing himself in 1794 as 'late common brewer' and possessing land, cash to the value of at least £1,400, a maidservant and a well-furnished house. There were apparently three generations of Robert Harrisons as brewers in Wakefield, all of whom were in affluent circumstances, and the last of whom gave up brewing about 1839 and henceforth lived the life of a gentleman.

What were apparently the beginnings of the tied-house system can be seen in connection with the Harrisons: a mortgage on a public house in the Softs at the bottom of Kirkgate in Wakefield was taken in 1798 and the *British Oak* in Kirkgate (previously dedicated as the

Figure 1. Invoice of 1864 from W Wigglesworth's Spring Brewery. *The John Goodchild Collection.*

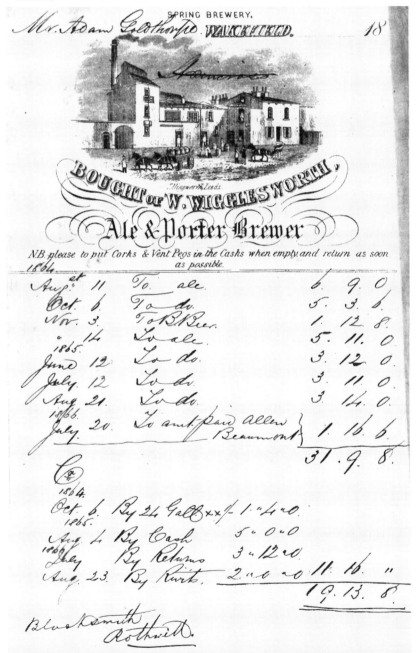

George and Dragon) was bought in 1839. The Harrisons' own brewery was in the Red Lion Yard, now Wild's Yard, in Kirkgate, and a further brewery, the Spring Brewery, was opened close by in Wild's Yard about 1850 by John Haigh and later run for many years by William Wigglesworth until its closure, as the Spring Brewery Co Ltd, in the 1890s (Figure 1).

A further firm of brewers, with William Young as principal, was advertising ale and porter in the local newspaper in 1820. Young seems to have been originally a maltster who turned to brewing later. The malt kilns and buildings in Pincheon Street occupied by Young and Becket were offered for sale in December 1820, but the partners had been brewing prior to that date in Park Brewery at Primrose Hill, advertising a reduction in prices in the January of that year. Young had a succession of partners, Thomas Becket dying in November 1823 and being succeeded as partner by T Pierson in January 1824. Young himself throve in his business and lived in the handsome (and then still rural) Grove House, Kirkgate, where he died in 1840 aged fifty-four. The business was then carried out for about a decade by John Young who gave it up about 1848 when a much more modern brewery, probably on a larger scale, had been started in the town.

In 1837 there were eighty-four inns, taverns and hotels in Wakefield and its suburbs, a number which had risen by thirteen in the previous fifteen years and which was to rise to 107 by 1870. There were also thirty-eight beerhouses in 1837. Probably most of the new public houses had no brewing apparatus and relied for their supplies of beer upon the breweries. This is borne out by the sale particulars of the second half of the century which show the newer inns – and now many of the older large town-centre houses too – having no brewhouse. There was thus an increasing demand for large-scale common brewing and in April 1845 the first steps were taken towards the provision of a large and modern brewery.

Thomas Mark Carter, a member of a family brewing at Knottingley from about 1806 (and until the end of the 1920s) and who had previously run a brewery in Dodworth Road, Barnsley, and later the Woolgreaves Brewery on a small rented estate in Sandal township, near Wakefield, purchased in April 1845 (along with the John Carter who had taken over the Knottingley brewery in 1836) land adjoining the Fairground Road, now known as part of George Street, in Wakefield. Later in the same year further and adjoining land was purchased. A brewery was built and probably brought into production in 1846. In 1851 there was a six hp steam engine in use at this brewery (Figures 2 and 3).

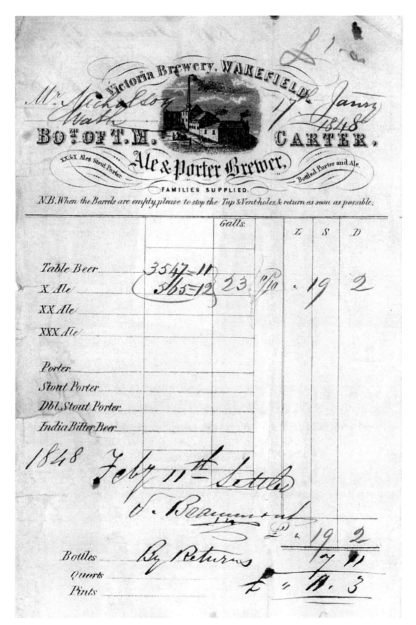

Figure 2. Invoice of 1848 from Thomas Carter's Victoria Brewery. *The John Goodchild Collection.*

Even while still at Woolgreaves Brewery, Carter had made arrangements to control an inn in George Street, Wakefield, and in 1846 he agreed to lease the *Jolly Sailor*, Thornes Lane (Figure 4). Carter was probably the first to develop the tied-house system on any scale in Wakefield – which of course secured beer outlets – although the system grew only slowly: in 1856 Carter owned only

Figure 3. Bill-head for Thomas Carter's Victoria Brewery. *The John Goodchild Collection.*

one inn actually in the town but by 1890 his firm owned ten inns and one beerhouse in Wakefield itself and controlled sixty-seven public houses altogether.

Carters prospered and they built a very substantial residence (probably in the 1850s) close to the brewery – a house which still exists today next to the Glad Tidings Hall. Later the brewery itself

Figure 4. The *Jolly Sailor*, Thornes Lane Wharf, in 2001. *Kate Taylor.*

was extended with a large warehouse and an ornamental arched and sculptured entrance (all of which existed until recent years) in Market Street. In the 1830s and 40s, Carter had been a partner in the firm of Carters and Smith of Sheffield and he later joined in other partnerships. His two sons, H M and Thomas Carter, joined him to form the firm of T H Carter and Sons and as such they worked the brewery at Wakefield, another at Burton-on-Trent, and a colliery at Allerton Bywater, near Castleford, from which, of course, coal supplies for brewing could be obtained. The father was a founder vice-president of the Wakefield Chamber of Commerce in 1864 and Mayor of Wakefield in 1857-58. His son, Alderman Thomas Carter JP, was later managing director of the Leeds and Wakefield Breweries Co Ltd, who took over the Wakefield Brewery in 1890. He died in 1895.

The growth of the significance of the common brewer is shown in the following table which relates to the Leeds excise collection area and includes Wakefield:

year	malt brewed and used by common brewers %	licensed victuallers	beerhouse brewers and others
1825	12	88	0
1851	33	47	20
1877	56	24	20
1892	64	18	18

and by 1872 only one Wakefield innkeeper is listed as brewing his own beer. The numbers of persons employed in common brewing also increased, the following being the Wakefield numbers:

1831 - 4 in 2 breweries
1841 - 10 in 4 breweries
1851 - 33 in 2 breweries
1861 - 45 in 4 breweries
1871 - 65 in 5 breweries

The number of breweries in Wakefield was to increase in the 1890s to a maximum of seven, decreasing to five in 1901, to four in 1922, to three in 1936 and to two in the 1960s after which for a time there were none. Some of the smaller and short-lived breweries are both difficult to document and of little significance, but some are worthy of at least an outline history. For example Jose Luis Fernandes and Co was in origin part of the Fernandes' empire in corn milling, wine merchanting, worsted spinning and coal-mining, which collapsed into bankruptcy in 1842. Re-started as a combined corn with

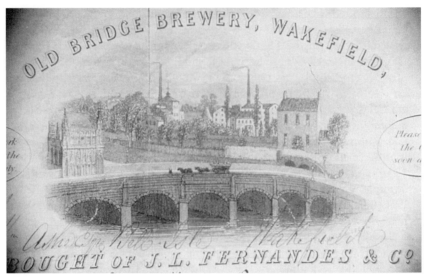

Figure 5. Bill-head for Fernandes' Brewery.

interests in milling, brewing and mining. In 1850 the Fernandes family had opened a brewery powered by a six hp steam engine and located alongside the Calder and Hebble's Fall Ing cut at Wakefield where the cut is crossed by the Wakefield and Weeland turnpike road, the adjoining bridge still being known colloquially as Fernandes Bridge (Figures 5 and 6) The partnership there of two Fernandes brothers, Jose Luis junior and Noel Luis, continued until 1881 when the junior partner took over the malting and brewing businesses and carried on the brewery until the time of the First World War.

Some of the Wakefield breweries were very small and apparently

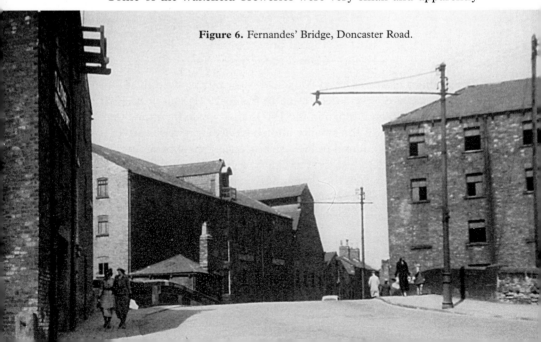

Figure 6. Fernandes' Bridge, Doncaster Road.

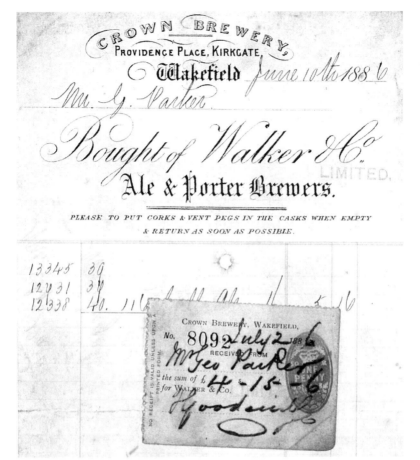

Figure 7. Receipted invoice of 1886 for the Crown Brewery. *The John Goodchild Collection.*

had very local markets. An example is John Hall's brewery at 29 Thornes Lane, which was at work in 1892 and 1897 but not earlier in 1887 or later in 1901. Another brewer was Charles Whiteley, who brewed in Westgate Common in 1887 but not in 1872 or in 1892. David Firth of the *White Horse* in Westgate was the only publican listed as being also a brewer in the directory of 1872.

Some breweries were a little larger: the Crown Brewery in Providence Place off Kirkgate, was opened in the early 1870s by George Newton, who presumably moved there at the end of his five-year lease of the Phoenix Brewery in Lower York Street, off Northgate, in 1870; he occupied the property for only a short time and for many more years the Phoenix was worked by Walker and Co, which had been founded in 1876 and became a limited liability company in 1886 with a capital of £50,000 at the beginning of the First World War but which closed down after that war (Figure 7).

The Phoenix Brewery in York Street, mentioned above, is the only

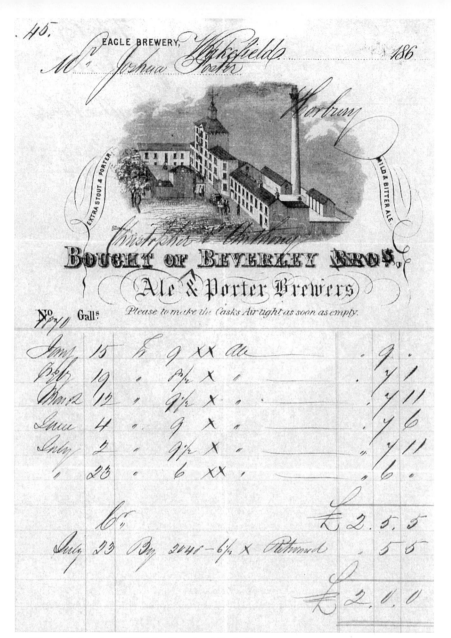

Figure 8. Invoice of 1870 for Beverleys' Eagle Brewery. *The John Goodchild Collection.*

small brewery in the area about which anything of the plant and machinery is known in detail: it was probably opened in 1860 although the site was conveyed to a common brewer in 1854 and was still owned by a brewer in 1878. The Phoenix, with its 'abundant supply of spring water' was advertised for sale in 1886. J & J Megsons' brewery in Back Lane in Wakefield was advertising ale and porter in 1838 and was advertised as to let in 1841; after his brother's death John Megson took a partner and it may have been a Megson interest which was involved in the Hagg Lane Brewery near the later Old Roundwood Colliery, which was advertised for sale in 1842.

The Eagle Brewery of Beverley Brothers, sited in Thornhill Street, dated from 1861 (said the late firm) or from 1863. The Beverley family had set up in Wakefield in the later 1840s as drapers, but two of the family started in business as brewers in the early 1860s and were leasing public houses in the area during that same decade. The business was converted to a limited

Figure 9. A Beverleys' beer mat. *The John Goodchild Collection.*

liability concern in 1888, with a capital in 1915-16 of £100,000. They worked the Eagle Brewery until the 1970s but curiously little is known of their history as so little documentation survives in relation to them (Figures 8-10).

The only other Wakefield brewery which existed as an actual brewing concern until the 1970s was to become ultimately one of the smallest independent breweries in the country in regard to both its output and the area occupied by the brewery; it was also the last

Figure 10. An advertisement of the 1930s for Beverleys. *The John Goodchild Collection.*

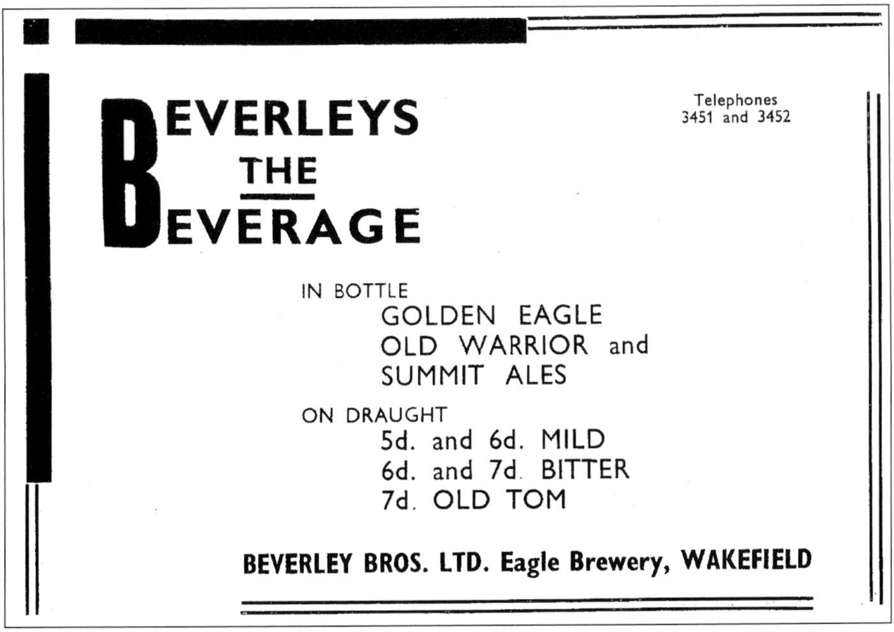

brewery to be established in Wakefield and its immediate district. Happily Westgate Brewery is well documented, at least in its earlier period. It dates from the commencement of the twentieth century when a company was got up by W H Kingswell senior, the Wakefield draper (and Mayor in 1908-09) and his family and by Mr John and Mrs M Horsfall. One H B Clark was engaged to brew and to manage the concern under a service agreement of January 1906. The capital was raised as follows:

	£
W H Kingswell and family	1090
John Horsfall and family	870
H B Clark	500
	£2460 in £1 shares

The minute amount of the capital will be noted, but the business managed to forge ahead slowly, with Kingswell as chairman and Clark as managing director. It seems possible that Clark had opened the brewery a little earlier than the date of the company's formal formation in March 1906 as beer duty was being paid from December 1905. The brewery site was purchased from Horsfall.

The first meeting of the new brewery company was held in March 1906 when chairman Kingswell reported that the concern had been duly registered, a company secretary had been appointed, solicitors and bankers nominated, a seal prepared, a clerk appointed (at 25 shillings a week), and arches under the nearby railway rented (Figure 11). Accounts were placed before the meeting and new casks were to be ordered – forty hogsheads, ten eighteen-gallons, twenty nine-gallons and twenty six-gallons. At the following meeting, in May, it was reported that a retail sales licence had been obtained and by April 1907 it was possible to declare a five per cent dividend. Beer output had been growing as the following three-monthly duty payments show:

Figure 11. Railway arches, Back Lane, Wakefield, in use in 2001 by Clark's Brewery. *Kate Taylor.*

	£	s	d
February 1906	105	15	9
July 1906	119	7	0
October 1906	161	4	0
January 1907	206	3	0

The company was in fact ultimately unsuccessful and eventually sold its interests, having agreed in 1912 to wind up and having dismissed H B Clark. A new company was formed in 1913 and continues to the present day although it ceased to produce beer – and was briefly the last Wakefield brewery to brew – in the early 1970s.

A long-lived brewery on the outskirts of Wakefield flourished at Calder Grove, close to transport facilities provided by turnpike, waterway and railway. Brewing was in existence here by the 1830s, when Thomas Bayldon was at work, and the business was carried on later by other Bayldons; ratebooks show that about 1858 the ownership of the property changed to Joseph Hammond and that he, George Spawforth and William Garthwaite were in partnership as brewers. Thomas Hammond, common brewer of Calder Grove, died in May 1919, aged eighty-nine, and the Oak Brewery is said to have closed in 1920 or 1921, having been carried on for a short period at the end of its life by John Garthwaite.

The end of the nineteenth century saw the larger regional and later the national breweries beginning to take an interest in the public houses of the Wakefield area. The Tadcaster Tower Brewery Company (which took up limited liability in 1894) had a depot in Wakefield in the 1880s and was leasing local pubs in the 1890s, while the amalgamation of Carters' Victoria Brewery with a Leeds brewery to form a larger concern in the 1890s has already been noted. Sykes and Co, of Dewsbury, founded in 1868 and centred latterly at the Soothill Brewery near Batley, became through amalgamations the Leeds and Batley Brewery Co Ltd in 1898 and possessed tied houses in various parts of Wakefield as well as in the Dewsbury area and in Leeds; in 1890 it leased seventy-six licensed premises to Ind, Coope and Co Ltd, of Romford and Burton on Trent, at a rental of £16,800, and thus another large brewery with national interests entered the local tied-house trade: the situation was soon to change radically in this direction.

Sources

Material in the John Goodchild Collection, Below Drury Lane Library, Wakefield.

12. THE ENCOURAGEMENT OF KINDLY INTERCOURSE: WAKEFIELD CHURCH INSTITUTION 1845-1930

by Kate Taylor

WAKEFIELD CHURCH INSTITUTION came into being at a public meeting held in the Court House on 24 October 1845.[1] The Vicar of Wakefield, Reverend Samuel Sharp, was in the chair and more than a dozen other Anglican clergy as well as some of the more prominent gentlemen of the town were in attendance. The principal speaker was Reverend Dr Scoresby, Vicar of Bradford, who had founded a Church Institution there in 1843.[2] The motion that 'an association be formed consisting of members of the Church of England in Wakefield to be called the Church Institution' was proposed by Reverend W T Alderson, the chaplain at Wakefield Prison, and was seconded by William Hey Dykes, manager of the Wakefield and Barnsley Union Bank. Dr Scoresby proposed the objects of the Institution:

> *The maintenance and advancement of the principles of the Church of England, the promotion of General Knowledge in subordination to religion, the cultivation of Church Music, and the encouragement of kindly intercourse among all classes of churchmen.*

The Bishop of Ripon, in whose diocese Wakefield then lay, was to be the Institution's patron, ex officio, and the Vicar of Wakefield its president. There were to be two secretaries, one a minister and one a layman. Reverend T B Parkinson, incumbent of the new ecclesiastical district of St Mary, was appointed as the former and J Rogers the latter. W H Dykes was elected as treasurer, and Mr Dibb as the librarian. Parkinson remained the clerical secretary until, and ironically, he defected to Rome in 1851.

But what prompted the founding of the Church Institution? Something of the motives can be gathered from the speeches at the inaugural event. Scoresby spoke of the value of imparting 'sound information' on

> *literary and scientific subjects in subordination to religion, which can alone render such knowledge conducive to the improvement of mankind*

and the promotion of their real, because their eternal, welfare.

This was a time when the Church was increasingly anxious that developments in our understanding of geology would not conflict with the understanding of the book of Genesis or, worse, foster atheism. But Scoresby also spoke of the ignorance, not least of the 'great distinctive principles of the Church of England', which led to people being 'seduced' by religious dissent and by Roman Catholicism.

But the Institution must have been founded, too, as a rival to the Wakefield Mechanics Institution the committee of which was dominated by men who were spiritually non-conformist and politically liberal.[3] Both bodies were prompted by the Victorian concern for 'rational recreation' and the 'civilising' of the working class.

Rooms were taken in a building lying between King Street and Wood Street and a library was swiftly established by transferring the 450 books that had earlier formed the library of the parish church. By February 1847 the library was open on Tuesday and Friday evenings from 7.00pm and the lecture room was available, as a reading room, on Tuesday, Wednesday, Friday and Saturday evenings from 7.30pm to 9.30pm. A choral society had been formed and there was a programme of fortnightly lectures on remarkably diverse topics. At the annual meeting of the Institution, Reverend W Cross, the second master at the Proprietary School, gave a talk on 'The actual and the ideal'; on 11 March Reverend Hugh B Smyth, vicar of Thornes, spoke on 'Historical characters in the time of Charles II' whilst on 29 April Robert Isaac Wilberforce (1802-1857, archdeacon of the East Riding and shortly to enter the Roman Catholic church) gave a talk on 'Astronomy'. General classes, supervised by a Mr Woodley, were said to be making 'slow, but it was hoped steady, progress'.[4] The Institution held a soiree in April when Reverend T B Parkinson read a letter from William Henry Leatham, who, he said, must be regarded as an independent judge, which was full of praise for the early success.

For a few years the Institution grew. A cricket club was formed in 1848 and the first branch, at Thornes, was founded in the same year

When a catalogue was issued in 1849 the library held more than 600 books. These included, as might be expected, volumes of sermons, works on church history, and theology, together with books on history, natural history, and travel. There were few novels – nothing, for example, by Jane Austen, the Brontes (*Jane Eyre, Agnes*

Grey and *Wuthering Heights* had been published in 1847), or Charles Dickens. There were, however, copies of Scott's novels; Defoe was represented by *Robinson Crusoe* but not, of course, *Moll Flanders*. There was Goldsmith's *Vicar of Wakefield* but none of his plays. Most interestingly considering its implicit threat to church doctrine, the library included a copy of Charles Darwin's *Journal of Researches into the Natural History and Geology of the Countries visited during the Voyage of HMS* Beagle. There was also Charles Lyell's *Principles of Geology, being an attempt to explain the former changes of the Earth's surface by reference to causes now in operation.* Next to Scott, the best represented author was Reverend William Gresley (1801-1876). Gresley was an ardent supporter of the Oxford movement. His work in the library included both historical novels (published in a series called 'The English Churchman') and a book simply entitled *Anglo-Catholicism*, as well as his (immensely popular in its day) *Principles of an English Churchman* (1838).[5]

Although the programme of lectures was always rather sparse, a leading actress of the time, Fanny Kemble, gave readings from Shakespeare in 1853.

By 1855 the leaders of the Institution were anxious to provide its own premises. £440 had been raised by subscription and on 19 May 1855 a building committee was appointed with powers to purchase a site, erect a building and draw up a trust deed. The sale of the Music Saloon in Wood Street seemed to provide a golden opportunity but it was acquired by the rival – and far more successful-body, the Mechanics Institution. Trustees for the proposed Church Institute were appointed at a further meeting on 3 September. They were Reverend Hugh Blagg Smyth (later to become vicar of Houghton Regis), Reverend John Bell, vicar of Rothwell and rural dean, Reverend John Sharp, incumbent of Horbury, Reverend Edward Twells, Reverend W T Alderson, Thomas Foljambe of Holmfield, Richard Dunn (corn merchant, living at Woolgreaves, Sandal), Edwin John Pickslay, John Maccabe (a bookseller), Ralph Linfield (an ironmonger), and John Connor (canal agent). By the end of the year the trustees had acquired a site in Marygate, then occupied by the manor bakehouse and adjoining living quarters, and a weighhouse, for £200.[6]

Plans were commissioned from William Dykes, architect son of W H Dykes, then practising in York. However in 1857 the adjoining property came on the market and was purchased on behalf of the trustees.

In June 1858, the four-storey premises until then occupied by the

Institution, forming one side of Crown Court, were destroyed by fire. The blaze destroyed the lecture room, news room, classrooms and library, now containing 1,400 books. It spread to an adjoining paper warehouse belonging to the bookseller, Mr Stanfield. A passing workman, a bill sticker, reported the fire to the police at 4.30am but it took forty-five minutes for the firemen to get water onto it and it was not until 7.00am that it was brought under control. A public meeting was held in the Girls' National School, Almshouse Lane, on 1 July to 'consider the best measures to be adopted with regard to the erection of new buildings for the use of the Institution in place of those destroyed by fire' and a resolution was passed unanimously that new premises be erected on the site already purchased.[7] But it was more easily said than done. Lack of finance and, apparently, misunderstandings between the trustees and the building committee, meant that it was still some years before work was to begin.

Meanwhile William Dykes, who had never fully recovered from the effects of falling through the ice on the river Ouse whilst attempting to rescue a friend, had died. New plans were commissioned from Alfred Burdekin Higham.[8] The foundation stone of the Institute was laid on 27 May 1861 by the Bishop of Ripon who had consecrated St Michael's Church a little earlier on the same day (Figure 1). The

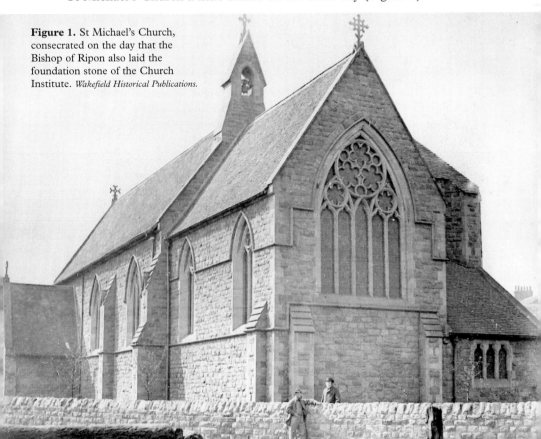

Figure 1. St Michael's Church, consecrated on the day that the Bishop of Ripon also laid the foundation stone of the Church Institute. *Wakefield Historical Publications.*

Figure 3. The view down Westgate from the Church Institute, a part of which is seen on the extreme right of the picture. *Wakefield Historical Publications.*

ceremony was preceded by a procession from St Michael's to Marygate. It included the scholars from the Green Coat school and pupils from schools attached to St John's, St Mary's, St Michael's and Holy Trinity churches.[9]

The Victorians seem to have loved bazaars! As a means of raising funds to pay for the building a bazaar was held in the Corn Exchange

in June.[10] It lasted five days. The first principle, in organising a bazaar, was to secure an impressive list of patrons. On this occasion they included the Countess of Harewood, The Earl of Dartmouth, the Earl of Mexborough, The Honorable and Reverend Philip Yorke Savile, Lady Pilkington, Lady Lister Kaye, Lord Wharncliffe, Colonel Smyth and the Honorable Mrs Smyth, and a string of local gentlemen and ladies. There were ten stalls, each under the wing of one of the leading ladies of the Wakefield establishment including Mrs Camidge (wife of the vicar of Wakefield), Mrs Kilby (wife of the vicar of St John's) and Miss Louisa Goodenough (granddaughter on one side of a bishop of Carlisle and on the other of an archbishop of York), then living at Heath and later to enter St Peter's Convent at Horbury. One wonders whether the over-crammed drawing rooms of Victorian society were stocked with items bought at such bazaars!

THE SIXTY-THIRD

ANNUAL REPORT

OF THE

Wakefield Church Institut

1908-9,

WITH LIST OF SUBSCRIBERS

AND

Members of Committee and Officers

For 1909-10.

Wakefield:

WEST YORKSHIRE PRINTING CO. LIMITED.

Figure 2. Wakefield Church Institute, which stood in Marygate, pictured on the cover the annual report for 1909-10. *Wakefield Library Headquarters, Local Studies Collection.*

Almost every stall had ottomans in sale. There were tables and chairs, some of the latter priced as high as £30. But there were also quantities of fire screens, hand screens, beadwork baskets, card baskets, vases, china, chair covers, doilies, wax flowers, items made in olive wood, and greenhouse plants.

Even this lavish event was not enough, however, to pay for the building. At the annual meeting in October 1861 a shortfall of £1,000 was reported.[11] Despite admitting that classes had 'fallen off for want of superintendence' and had not been renewed, the report was generally a positive one: membership had increased by eighty-six and the Penny Bank was prospering. The News Room had been incorporated with a defunct subscription newsroom in Wood Street.

The gothic-style Institute, built by Edward Latham in red brick and with a spire, was opened on 22 June 1862[12]. (Figures 2 and 3) It had a news room, a library, a lecture hall capable of seating 500, class rooms, an entrance hall and a picture gallery. The evening began with a service at 7.00pm conducted by the vicar of Wakefield, followed by a rendering of Handel's *Hallelujah Chorus*. There were then congratulatory speeches and further music from the choir which had been brought together for the event by J Emmerson and E O Dykes, another son of the bank manager.

Railings were added to the front of the building in 1863-4. Already in 1865 the building was giving cause for concern as the beams supporting the lecture room had begun to sag and it was necessary to lay a new floor.

With its own premises the committee arranged a full programme of weekly lectures for the 1962-3 winter season. The advertisement for these, which appeared in October, announced meetings of the Chess Club and promised that evening classes were being formed. These were established during the 1863-4 year. An advertisement on 8 October 1864 in the *Wakefield Free Press* shows that there was a class on Tuesday and Friday evenings for young men wishing to learn to read, write and cope with arithmetic, at 2d a week, and a class in 'phonography' (shorthand) on Tuesdays at five shillings for the course.

In 1863-4 the Institution took over a branch of Mudie's library formerly run at Hicks and Allens.

Lectures continued on a somewhat random and ad hoc basis for some years. Among them in the 1865-6 season was one by Reverend John Bacchus Dykes, yet another son of William Hey Dykes and the composer of numerous well-known hymn tunes, on the history of English church music.[13]

The main sources of income for the Institution were from subscriptions and the annual soiree. There were four classes of subscription. For the highest, a guinea, one was entitled to bring two ladies to lectures and concerts, or to bring two men provided that they were not residents of Wakefield. For 10s 6d one could bring two ladies or one man. The 5s (25p) subscription entitled one to bring only two ladies. There was a subscription of 2s 6d (12.5p) for minors but they could not bring guests at all.

A soiree is defined simply as an evening party at which one listens, dances or sings. The Church Institution soirees certainly involved a good deal of listening as the president and others gave reports of the year's activities and the general state of the Institution, perhaps because so few people attended the annual meetings. They were held in the Corn Exchange, either on the draughty floor of the exchange room itself, or upstairs in the saloon. Refreshments were in the form of tea, buns and cakes. The custom was for ladies, including wives of the vicar of Wakefield and other principal Anglican townsmen, to bring 'trays', presumably loaded with the food.

A programme for the soiree on 28 January 1886 shows something of the length of the event.[14] Doors opened at 4.30pm and tea was on the tables at 5.00pm, but it was not until 7.00pm that the president, then Canon Norman Straton, took the chair. The concert was scheduled to begin at 7.30pm and featured the band of the 15th (the King's) Hussars with solos by Florence Hallowell. The words of Miss Hallowell's songs - typical Victorian sentimentality, mingled with melodrama and patriotism, are given in the programme. Fred Brown's *I'll be a soldier, Mother*, with its strained syntax and forced rhymes, provides a sample:

> *What will you be, my darling? what will my bonnie boy be?*
> *When childhood days are over with all their mirth and glee.*
> *I'll be a soldier, mother, when I a man am grown,*
> *And father's sword you'll give me to be my very own.*
> *I long to be a soldier, and wish the time would come,*
> *When I could wear a red coat and march behind the drum.*
>
> *Oh, say not so my darling! oh, say not so my boy!*
> *You'd wring my heart with anguish, and all my hopes destroy,*
> *For darling 'twas in battle, your own dear father fell,*
> *And you, my only treasure, I cannot spare as well.*
> *But mother, dearest mother, I've often heard you say*
> *You pray'd that I'd grow like father, and be like him some day.*
>
> *Within the mother's heart then did duty strive with love,*
> *She pray'd that light to guide her might fall from heav'n above,*
> *That in the coming future, she might at honour's call,*
> *Bid farewell to her darling, and trust Him who rules over all.*

In addition to the soiree, the Institution for some years held an annual service, on All Saints Day.

Annual meetings could be fraught affairs. Some members could not resist making points of order, for example, as when in 1865 it was argued that a member of the committee could not move the adoption of the annual report. The meeting of 1868 was described in the local press as 'stormy'.[15] The previous year had not been very successful; there had been losses on lectures and concerts; the Institution now had a deficit of £138 compared with one of £75 on the previous year; there was a quarrel as to whether the vicar of Wakefield should remain president ex-officio or stand for re-election annually; and there was some debate as to whether the rules had been altered or not. Matthew Hick complained that the committee was unwieldy and that it was entirely wrong that every clergyman who was a member of the Institution should have an automatic right to be on it. A Mr Gemmell described the affairs as an 'unmitigated muddle'.[16]

It would be tedious to relate the fortunes of the Institution and its building over the next decades. Suffice it to say that its debts never lessened! Moreover the evening classes, principally in basic education, which had been regarded as so important at its foundation, were never very successful and, following the 1870 Education Act, became steadily less required. Perhaps it was always something of a white elephant! Nonetheless at the time of its diamond jubilee in 1905 the Institution was described as having:

> constantly and consistently rendered its quiet, steady, and invaluable services to the Church of England.

It was then (and perhaps for years earlier) run by a general committee with three sub-committees: a lecture, library and news-room committee, a house and finance committee, and an SPCK committee.[17]

In the early years of the twentieth century the financial position of the Institution grew steadily worse. A table drawn up in 1907 shows a decline in income from subscriptions from £132 16s 10d (£132 84p) in 1901-02 to £110 1s 3d (£110 6.5p) in 1905-06. At the same time income from lettings dropped from £58 7s (£58 35p) in 1901-2 to £43 4s (£43 20p) in 1905-6. But the wages for the caretaker had risen from £38 1s (£38 5p) to £42 9s 6d (£42 47.5p) Lettings were adversely affected by the availability of the Cathedral Chapter House for small meetings which had earlier been held at the Institute; the Chapter House formed a part of the extension to the Cathedral built as a memorial to Wakefield's first bishop, William Walsham How, and opened in 1905. Two lectures in 1905 by the Bishop of Bristol, on Early Church History in England as read from our most Ancient Monuments, were given in the gymnasium at the Girls' High School. Then at some time prior to 1906 the Cathedral had opened a Mission Room at 158 Westgate (below the *Swan with Two Necks*) and here, too, some meetings took place. The opening of the vast extensions to the Wakefield Industrial Co-operative Society buildings in Westgate also provided alternative meeting rooms in the Unity and Minor Halls. There was a modest profit on goods sold on behalf of SPCK but the association with Mudie's library was, by 1906, operating on a loss with an income of £11 11 3d (£11 56p) in subscriptions against a cost of £12 14s 9d (£12 74p) for carriage and for the subscriptions to Mudie's itself.[18] Moreover most members chose to pay the minimum annual subscription of only seven shillings whilst the number of those paying a guinea declined. No doubt in an effort to attract more members the 1905 annual meeting decided to admit all Church Sunday School teachers and all teachers in National Schools in the Wakefield deanery at a reduced subscription of 5s (25p). However the accounts for 1905-6 show only four subscriptions at that level.

In 1906-7 the Institution was affiliated to the newly-formed Wakefield Educational Guild.[19] In May 1907, when the Institute's deficit stood at some £40 Archdeacon Donne wrote to Herbert Beaumont suggesting that the Institute be sold and the proceeds devoted to the needs of Church schools.[20] In its report for 1908-9 the committee pleaded for an increase in the numbers subscribing to the Institution and acknowledged that their members held themselves responsible for the, by then substantial, bank overdraft. Their task of raising funds had been the more difficult, they said, since they would be competing for money with the Church schools, for which an appeal had recently been launched. Attendance at lectures had been disappointing.

Topical matters affecting the Church of England were occasions for debates. In January 1906 there was a debate on Sunday Observance. A fortnight later the Institute hall was filled for a debate on Church Patronage. On 24 January 1907 the members of church debating societies in Wakefield met on the question 'Should the laity have increased powers in Church matters?' On 18 February of the same year Chancellor Smith spoke prior to a discussion on the Report of the Ritual Commission.

A depot of the Church of England Temperance Society was opened at the Institute in 1907 and the publications and badges of the Society were sold at there.

The Institute hall was in 1908-9 let not only to numerous church organizations such as the Society for the Propagation of the Gospel in Foreign Parts, the Church of England Temperance Society, and the Additional Curates' Society, but also to voluntary groups including the Education Guild, the Froebel Society, the Philharmonic Society, the Paxton Society, the Deaf and Dumb Society, and the Provident and Perseverance Friendly Societies. But these lettings never brought in sufficient income to keep the enterprise afloat. For just a few years more it ploughed on. In May 1910 Reverend J T Levens, the clerical secretary, wrote indicating that the committee were planning to convert a part of the basement into a shop.[21] The building was also used for auction sales; Saville and Kilburn sold the furniture from Haverland House there in October 1910. (Figure 4) It was still being used on occasions for auctions by Ernest W Glover in 1930.

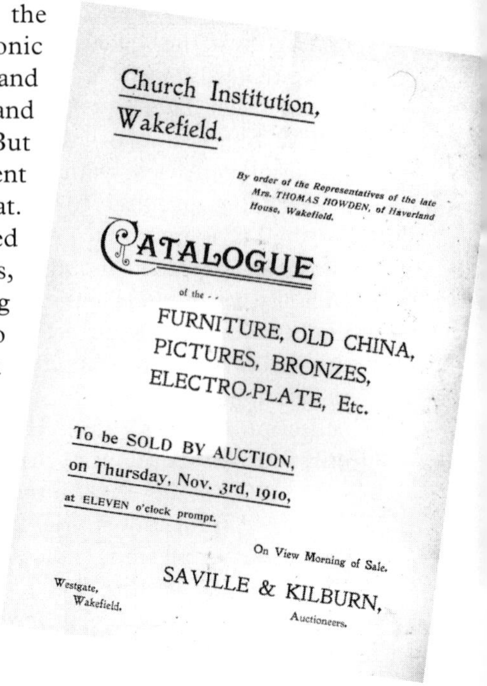
Church Institution,
Wakefield.

By order of the Representatives of the late Mrs. THOMAS HOWDEN, of Haverland House, Wakefield.

CATALOGUE
of the . .
FURNITURE, OLD CHINA,
PICTURES, BRONZES,
ELECTRO-PLATE, Etc.

To be SOLD BY AUCTION,
on Thursday, Nov. 3rd, 1910,
at ELEVEN o'clock prompt.

On View Morning of Sale.

SAVILLE & KILBURN,
Auctioneers.

Westgate,
Wakefield.

Figure 4. Catalogue for an auction at the Church Institute in 1910. *Wakefield Library Headquarters, Local Studies Collection.*

At the annual meeting in 1910, when an overdraft of £246 was reported, the committee recommended that the Institution be wound up but the proposal was defeated and an ad hoc group was set up to find a new scheme to prolong its life. Fred Simpson, a local architect was called to advise on ways of adapting the building, including establishing a billiard room, but the cost was way beyond the Institution's means. The newsroom and library closed in May 1911.[22]

In 1912, when it was said that the Institute as it had been run ' was obviously out of date and out of touch with modern churchfolk', efforts were made to rescue it as a Church Club. The Cathedral branch of the Church of England Men's Society, which had been founded in March 1909, formed a committee and arranged with the Institute Committee to take the building over for a three year period.[23] Meanwhile the building continued to provide a venue for local organisations such as the Paxton Society and the Photographic Society.

At some time during the First World War the Institute became the headquarters of the Wakefield Women Workers' League. On 24 July 1918 this body, led by Mrs Edwin Hirst, opened it as a Sailors and

Figure 5. The site of the Church Institute, Marygate, in 2001. *Kate Taylor.*

Soldiers Club for the wounded servicemen stationed in the military hospitals in or near Wakefield. They provided a reading room, a canteen and a room fitted with three billiard tables. The upstairs hall was to serve as a concert room. The opening was performed by the then mayor, Councillor G Blakey.[24]

Information about the fortunes of the Institute for the next years is sparse. When Wakefield Historical Society was formed in 1924, its early committee meetings were held there, at Webster's cafe or at the Music Saloon, and some of its first lectures were given at the Institute. On 6 March 1925 Mr Milner gave a lecture there on Old Wakefield.

In 1930 the Institute was sold by the then trustees, Charles William Fennell, Edward Milnes (the printer), Harry Broadbent (a joiner) Albert Edward Jones, Albert Edward Darling (a local government officer), W H Coles (the solicitor and Diocesan Registrar). David Frederick Martin (a draper), and Edward Scott Perkin (a jeweller). It was bought by F W T Mills, an accountant and sometime mayor of Wakefield, and his associate, Alan Greasby.[25] From then on it was known as the Central Premises, or Central Hall.

Owned in 1945 by Jock Ltd, it came up for auction and was bought by Wakefield Corporation for £5,748 10s. The basement shop was let to F Wilkinson for his hairdressing business, but the main premises were taken over by the Education Department as the central youth headquarters and became known as Church House.[26] Local authorities had become responsible for providing a youth service under an Act of Parliament of 1940. As Youth House the Institute provided offices, two meeting rooms (one of which doubled as a canteen), a kitchen and the hall. A stage was erected in the hall with the profits from the Pageant of Youth which was staged at Wakefield's Theatre Royal and Opera House in 1947.[27]

But even as Youth House, the Church Institute was a liability. It closed in the early 1970s and was demolished to be replaced by a row of shops (Figure 5).

Notes and References

1. R Phipps, *A Brief Sketch of the History and Work of the Wakefield Church Institute from October 1845 to January 1896* (1896); *Wakefield Journal*, 28 November 1845.
2. William Scruton, *Pen and Pencil Pictures of Old Bradford*, (1890), reprinted 1985, p88.
3. Clifford Brook, 'Wakefield Mechanics Institution', *Wakefield Historical Society Journal*, Vol 6 (1979).
4. *Wakefield Journal*, 11 February 1847.
5. *Dictionary of National Biography*.
6. Declaration of Trust of 13 December 1855, the John Goodchild Collection.
7. *Wakefield Journal*, 2 July 1858.
8. E R Kelly (Ed) *The Post Office Directory of the West Riding of Yorkshire*, 1867, p1007.
9. *Wakefield Express*, 1 June 1861
10. *Ibid*. 8 June 1861.
11. *Wakefield Journal*, 4 October 1861.
12. *Ibid*. 30 June 1862.
13. Poster in the John Goodchild Collection.
14. Programme in the John Goodchild Collection.
15. *Wakefield Journal*, 9 October 1868.
16. *Wakefield Express*, 10 October 1868.
17. Annual report 1905-6, Wakefield District Library Service, local studies collection, Balne Lane, Wakefield.
18. Documents in the John Goodchild Collection.
19. Annual report in the John Goodchild Collection.
20. Letter in the John Goodchild Collection.
21. Another letter in the John Goodchild Collection.
22. *Wakefield Express*, 20 January 1912.
23. *Ibid*, 4 April 1912; the Cathedral Magazine June 1909.
24. *Wakefield Express*.
25. Wakefield Registry of Deeds.
26. Minutes, Wakefield County Borough Council 1945-6.
27. *In the Service of Youth*, pamphlet in the Wakefield District Library Service local studies collection, Balne Lane Library.

Wakefield Yards: Appendix to Chapter One

	Yard Name	No	Location	Census	YR.BK	Roll	Diry	Map
1	Akeds		Westgate					1851
2	Albion	106	Kirkgate	1851	1872	1868	1857	1851
3	Albion		Northgate					
4	Albion (Hotel)		Westgate	1891			1887	
5	Albion Mill		Ings Rd	1891				
6	Aldens/Aldams		Kirgate					1851
7	Allatt's		Kirgate	1891			1887	
8	Alverthorpe Brick			1851				
9	Ambrose		Kirgate				1847	
10	Armitage	N/S	Charles St to Tavern St	1891			1822	1823
11	Armitage		Park St	1851				
12	Ashes		Belle Vue	1891				
13	Ashton's	49	Westgate End	1891			1892	
14	Avison	156	Kirgate	1851	1872		1862	
15	Bakehouse		William St	1851			1837	
16	Baker's	80	Kirgate	1851	1872		1842	
17	Baker's	13	William St				1922	
18	Balinforths		Kirgate	1851				
19	Balne				1851			
20	Barcroft prob Bencroft		Kirgate	1891				
21	Barff's		Westgate					1823
22	Barker's		Kirgate	1851				1851
23	Barraclough's		Kirgate				1837	
24	Barratt's	86	Northgate	1851	1872	1850	1837	1851
25	Barratt's Upper		Northgate			1851		
26	Batty's	24	William St				1922	
27	Baxendale's	141	Kirgate	1881			1904	
28	Beaumont's	83	Kirgate	1851	1872	1852	1842	
29	Beaumont's		Thornes	1881				
30	Bee Hive	44	Kirgate	1851		1850	1837	
31	Beever's		Westgate					1823
32	Belle Isle		Barnsley Rd	1881				
33	Belle Isle Malt Kiln			1891				
34	Bell's		Grove St	1891				
35	Bell's	82	Northgate	1891			1887	
36	Bell's		Westgate				1830	1823
37	Bencroft	112	Kirgate	1891			1861	
38	Bern's		Kirgate	1851				
39	Berry's		Providence St	1891			1830	
40	Binn's		Thornes	1881				
41	Binton's			1851				
42	Black Horse		Westgate	1851			1887	
43	Black Lion		Kirgate to the Springs					1851
44	Black Swan	2	Silver St	1851	1872	1852	1822	1851
45	Blackburn's		Eastmoor	1891				
46	Blackburn's		Kirgate	1851			1887	
47	Blackburn's		Market St	1851				
48	Black's or Day's		Kirgate			1860		
49	Blacksmith			1881				
50	Blakey's	E/S	Kirgate	1851				
51	Blue Bell		Westgate					1823
52	Boiler		Westgate End	1891				
53	Bolland's		Warrengate			1863	1887	
54	Bolton's		Providence St	1891				
55	Bouchier		Kirgate	1891	1915			
56	Bramham	146-168	Stanley Rd	1881	1872		1887	
57	Brett's			1891				
58	Brewer's Arms	162	Westgate	1851			1904	
59	Brewery		Doncaster Rd	1891				
60	Brewery	40	Kirgate				1892	
61	Brick		Pincheon St				1887	
62	Bricklayer's Tavern		Kirgate					1851
63	Brickmaker	42	Stanley Rd/Greenhill Rd	1891	1872		1887	
64	Bridge			1881				
65	Brigg's	102	Northgate	1891			1887	
66	Brigg's		Westgate	1891			1837	
67	Brigg's	5-13	Park St				1908	
68	Brisco's		Westgate					1851
69	Britannia	31	Warrengate	1891			1922	
70	British Oak	114	Kirgate				1862	
71	Brook's		Westgate				1837	1823
72	Brook's		Westgate					1823
73	Bull & Mouth		Kirgate	1881			1862	
74	Bull see GT Bull							
75	Bull see Littel Bull			1851				

	Yard Name	No	Location	Census	YR.BK	Roll	Diry	Map
76	Burdekins		Providence St	1851				
77	Burrell's		Westgate	1851	1851		1837	1851
78	Burton's		Westgate			1850	1830	
79	Butcher's Arm	79	Stanley Rd	1881			1908	
80	Cain's		Westgate	1851	1872			1851
81	Calder & Hebble		Bridge St	1851				
82	Camplin	94	Stanley Rd	1851	1872		1887	
83	Canal		Bridge St				1887	
84	Carabine's		Westgate	1881				
85	Carkes?			1891				
86	Carksons?			1891				
87	Carr's		Westgate					1823
88	Cass	150	Kirkgate	1851	1872	1860	1887	1851
89	Cement Yard		?Ings Road	1881				
90	Chadwick's	88	Kirkgate				1908	
91	Challengers		Westgate	1851				
92	Chapel		Stanley	1851	1872		1887	
93	Chemical			1881				
94	Church		Northgate	1851			1830	1823
95	Clayton	121	Stanley Rd		1872		1837	
96	Clayton's		Doncaster Rd, nr White Bear	1891			1922	
97	Clayton's		Eastmoor	1891				
98	Clayton's		South St	1851		1850		
99	Cock & Swan		Westgate	1851	1872	1850	1822	1823
100	Cock Inn		Batley Rd		1915			
101	Colour Works			1881				
102	Cook's		Kirgate					1823
103	Cooling		Kirgate			1860	1875	
104	Coolings		Horbury Rd		1872			
105	Co-operative		Alverthorpe	1891				
106	Cooper's Arms		Westgate				1853	1823
107	Cowell's		Northgate				1837	
108	Craven's		Kirgate	1851				
109	Cross Pipe's		Alverthorpe	1891				
110	Crossland's		Kirkgate				1837	
111	Crown & Anchor		Kirkgate				1887	1857
112	Crowther's		Westgate				1830	1823
113	Curtis		Kirkgate			1854		
114	Cutter			1881				
115	Day		Kirkgate		1872	1850	1887	
116	Day's	E/S	Kirkgate	1881				
117	Day's		Northgate				1887	
118	Deacon's Warehouse			1851				
119	Dibb's		Providence St	1851				
120	Dickenson		South St	1891				
121	Dickenson's	21	Pincheon St	1891	1915			
122	Dispensary	47	Northgate	1881	1872		1853	
123	Dixon's	158	Kirkgate	1881			1904	
124	Dixon's		Westgate					
125	Dog		Westgate				1861	
126	Dolphin		Kirkgate					
127	Domfritt's		Kirkgate					1851
128	Dr Crowther's		Northgate					1823
129	Dr Kemp's		Alverthorpe	1881				
130	Dragon see Green		Westgate					
131	Dudley		Belle Vue	1891				
132	Dudley		Clarion St		1915			
133	Duncan		Thornes Ln	1881	1872			
134	Dusty Miller see Old							
135	Dyehouse		Flanshaw Lane	1881				
136	Dyehouse		Thornes	1881				
137	Dyehouse			1851				
138	Dyson's		Kirkgate				1842	
139	Elephant & Castle	107	Westgate				1857	1823
140	Ellarby's		Thornes	1891				
141	Elwick		Northgate				1853	
142	Elwick & Robinsons		Northgate			1850		
143	Errick		Wood St				1857	
144	Farrar's	21	Pincheon St	1881			1908	
145	Fawcett's	167	Kirkgate	1891	1872	1850	1837	1851
146	Fennell's	31	Westgate	1851			1887	
147	Fenton Heald's	132	Kirkgate	1851	1915		1908	
148	Fernandes		Kirkgate				1887	1823
149	Firth	61-69	Stanley Rd	1851	1873			
150	Firth's	c18	Ingwell St	1881			1887	1851
151	Fleece	c41	Brook St				1922	
152	Fleece		Market Place	1851			1830	1823
153	Fleece		Westgate				1822	
154	Fox & Grapes	c99	Jacob's Well Ln				1904	

	Yard Name	No	Location	Census	YR.BK	Roll	Diry	Map
55	Fox's or Foxes		Lord Rodney Yard					
56	Fryer's	46	Northgate	1881			1904	
57	Gas House	15	Warrengate	1881	1872	1850	1847	
58	George & Crown	2	Silver St to Chanery Ln	1851	1872	1850	1834	1823
59	George Hotel		Kirkgate					1823
60	Gilderdale's		Northgate					1823
61	Gill's	51	Northgate to Bond Terr	1881	1872	1850	1853	1851
62	Gill's		Strafford Square				1887	
63	Glass Works			1891				
64	Glass House			1881				
65	Globe (Inn)	c169	Westgate	1881	1872		1875	
66	Gloders?		Alverthorpe	1891				
67	Glovers		Thornes	1891				
68	Golden Lion	16	Kirkgate		1903			
69	Golden Lion		Westgate				1861	1851
70	Gosnay		Eastmoor	1891				
71	Governor's		Northgate	1881	1872		1887	
72	Governor's	168	Stanley Rd	1881			1887	
73	Great Bull		Westgate			1850	1837	1823
74	Greave's		Denby Dale Rd	1891	1915			
75	Green Dragon		Westgate	1851	1872	1850		1823
76	Green's Foundry		Calder Vale Road					
77	Haigh & Graham's Wood		George St					1823
78	Haigh's		Westgate					1851
79	Haigh's Low	S/S	Charles St	1891			1909	
80	Haigh's Top	S/S	Charles St	1891			1908	
81	Haldane's		Kirkgate	1851				
82	Halliday		Greenhill Rd	1891	1872			
83	Hall's		Thornes	1891				
84	Hammond	170	Kirkgate	1851	1872			
85	Hampshire's		Warrengate	1891	1903		1904	
86	Hanson's		Kirkgate				1837	
87	Harewood Arms		Kirkgate				1857	1851
88	Harrisons	166	Kirkgate	1851			1837	1823
89	Hartley's	176	Kirgate	1851	1872		1837	1823
90	Hartley's		Westgate	1881				1823
91	Hastings			1891				
92	Hattersley's		Charles St	1851				
93	Haworth's	82	Westgate				1904	
94	Hawshaws		South St	1891				
95	Heald's		Kirkgate		1872		1837	
96	Hebble		Flanshaw Lane	1881				
97	Hesling's	c24	Charles St				1908	
98	Hodgson's		?Westgate	1851				
99	Holdsworth's		Doncaster Rd, nr White Bear	1891			1922	
100	Holdsworth's		Providence St		1915			
101	Holdswoth's		Westgate					1823
102	Holt's		Westgate	1881	1915			
103	Horner's	108	Kirkgate	1851	1872		1837	1823
104	Horn's		South St	1891		1850		
105	Howarth's		Kirkgate	1891			1887	
106	Howden's	230	Kirkgate				1892	1851
107	Howson's?			1851				
108	Hudson's	5-21	Pincheon				1908	
109	Hudson's		Savile St				1904	
110	Hudson's		Stanley Rd	1881			1908	
111	Hurst's		Westgate					1823
112	Ings Mill			1881				
113	Ingwell	173	Kirkgate	1851	1872		1837	1851
114	Irwin's		Kirkgate					1823
115	Ives		Batley Rd		1915			
116	Jackson's		Northgate		1960			
117	Jackson's		Kirkgate					
118	Jacques		Charles St	1851				
119	Jennings		Thornes	1881				
120	Johnson's	c10	Charles St	1891			1922	
121	Jolly Sailor						1862	
122	Jubb		Thornes	1881				
123	Kay		Warrengate					1851
124	Keddy's		Kirkgate	1891				1851
125	Kemps		Alverthorpe Rd				1887	
126	Kershaw's		Providence St	1851				
127	Kings Head		Kirkgate	1881			1887	
128	Kirkhamgate		Alverthorpe	1881				
129	Kitsons			1881				
130	Knowles		Kirkgate	1881			1887	
131	Lake Yard			1891				
132	Lancaster		Kirkgate				1887	
133	Land		Northgate	1851	1872		1892	
134	Land's	c84	Kirkgate			1861		

	Yard Name	No	Location	Census	YR.BK	Roll	Diry	Map
235	Lascelles		Kirkgate			1850		
236	Laycock	100	Kirkgate		1872		1857	1851
237	Laycock		Westgate to Ltl Bull Yd	1851	1872	1850	1822	1823
238	Leatham's		Westgate					1823
239	Lee's		Kirkgate	1851		1850	1830	1823
240	Leopard		Kirkgate	1851	1872		1837	
241	Library	98	Northgate	1851	1872			
242	Little Bull	23	Westgate	1851	1872	1852	1847	1823
243	Lord Rodney see Rodney							
244	Lowries	33	Northgate	1891	1872			
245	Lund's		Northgate			1860		
246	Major Burton's		Westgate					1823
247	Manchester		Kirkgate					1823
248	Manor House	18	Kirkgate	1851		1850	1837	1851
249	Marshall's		Westgate	1851		1850	1842	1852
250	Mellard's		Kirkgate				1857	
251	Mellor's		Kirkgate	1851		1856	1866	
252	Messon's		Belle Vue	1891				
253	Midwoods			1881				
254	Mill	c44	Ingwell St				1908	
255	Mill		Thornes Lane					
256	Milnthorpe's		Kirkgate					1851
257	Milson		Thornes	1881				
258	Mitchells		Alverthorpe Rd	1881			1887	
259	Model	33	Warrengate	1897			1922	
260	Mollacrees	94	Kirkgate	1851	1872		1922	
261	Monk's		Monk St				1887	
262	Moorcock		Kirkgate					1851
263	Moorhouse		Northgate				1887	
264	Morgan's		Kirkgate				1862	
265	Mosley's		Kirkgate				1887	
266	Moxon's		Kirkgate	1881			1887	
267	Murgatroyd		Kirkgate	1881			1892	
268	Murgatroyd	7-27	Park Lodge Ln				1908	
269	Museum		Northgate	1851				
270	Navigation	261	Kirkgate	1851	1872	1852	1887	
271	Navigation Warehouse					1856		
272	Naylor's		Westgate					1823
273	Nelson		Belle Vue	1881				
274	Nelson's	12	Park St				1904	
275	New Dusty Miller	c10	Charles St				1908	
276	New Elephant		Corn Market/New St				1830	
277	New Inn		Thornes	1891				
278	Noel		Kirkgate					
279	Norman		Eastmoor	1891				
280	Northorps		William St	1891	1915			
281	Number One		Kirkgate					
282	Oates	163	Kirkgate	1851			1887	
283	Old Church					1850	1822	
284	Old Crown	32	Northgate	1851	1872	1850	1822	1851
285	Old Dusty Miller		Kirkgate					
286	Old Foundry		Ossett Rd			1852	1834	
287	Old Globe see Globe			1891				
288	Old Green Dragon	130	Westgate				1857	1851
289	Old Library		Northgate					1851
290	Old Post Office		Bull Ring		1872			
291	Old Red Lion		Kirkgate				1830	1823
292	Old Ship Inn		See Ship					
293	Old Waggon Warehouse					1850	1887	
294	Old Warehouse		Westgate	1891	1872	1850		
295	Old Wharf						1837	
296	Oldroyd's				1915		1842	
297	Ough's		Park St	1891				
298	Oxford		?Kirkgate	1881				
299	Oxley's				1838		1837	
300	Parkin ?Perkin			1891				
301	Pearson's		Warrengate	1881				
302	Perkins		Northgate			1860		
303	Perkins		Westgate					1851
304	Phoenix			1881				
305	Pilkington's	E/S	Denby Dale Rd	1881			1922	
306	Pitt's		Kirkgate				1857	
307	Playhouse		Westgate			1832	1822	1823
308	Plumpton		Westgate End	1891				
309	Post Office		Market Place				1857	1823
310	Postman (Inn)	78	Northgate	1851		1850	1837	1851
311	Potter's		Northgate					1823
312	Priestley's		Northgate	1851			1857	
313	Priest's		Alverthorpe	1891				
314	Prince's		Westgate	1881				

	Yard Name	No	Location	Census	YR.BK	Roll	Diry	Map
315	Prince's see Princess		Kirkgate		1872			
316	Princess	36	Kirkgate	1851	1903		1862	1851
317	Prospect		Westgate	1851	1872	1850	1834	1851
318	Providence		Alverthorpe	1891				
319	Quaker		Belle Vue	1891				
320	Quaker House		Doncaster Rd		1915			
321	Queens Arms	89	Kirkgate				1892	
322	Queens Arms		Thornes	1891				
323	Railway		Black Ln	1881			1927	
324	Rawling	N/S	Greenhill Rd	1851	1872		1887	
325	Rayner's		South St	1891				
326	Rayner's		Westgate	1881				1823
327	Rayner's (2)		Westgate					1823
328	Red Lion		Kirkgate	1851	1872	1850	1830	
329	Rhodes		Eastmoor	1881				
330	Rhodes	81	Kirkgate	1881	1872		1875	
331	Rhode's	21	Pincheon St				1908	
332	Rhode's		Warrengate			1850		
333	Rishworth's		Westgate					1823
334	Robert's		South St			1850	1887	
335	Robin Hood	28-54	Horbury Rd	1891			1904	
336	Robinson		Northgate		1872	1850	1830	
337	Robinson's		Barnsley Rd		1915			
338	Robinson's		Westgate					
339	Robson's		Cross Hatfield St				1887	
340	Robsons		Westgate	1851	1872	1834	1830	1823
341	Rodley			1891				
342	Rodney	5	Westgate	1851	1872	1850	1830	1823
343	Royal Oak		Warrengate		1903			
344	Saville			1891				
345	Saw	27	Westgate to Geo St	1851	1872	1850	1822	1823
346	Schofield's		Westgate	1981	1915			
347	Scott's	c4	John St	1851			1922	
348	Scott's	114	North Westgate		1872	1850	1837	1823
349	Scott's		South Westgate	1881				1851
350	Selby's		Kirgate					1823
351	Seller's	130	Stanley Rd	1851	1872			
352	Shackleton's						1822	
353	Sharp's		Back Lane				1834	
354	Sharp's		Northgate				1834	
355	Shaw	63	Northgate to Gills Yd	1851	1873	1850	1837	1823
356	Shaw's	25	Kirkgate	1891			1837	
357	Shaw's		Westgate	1881				
358	Shear		Northgate				1867	1823
359	Shift		Kirkgate	1851				
360	Shilletts		Northgate				1904	
361	Shillito		Northgate		1915			
362	Ship	214	Kirkgate	1851	1872	1850	1857	1851
363	Shires		Stanley Road	1891				
364	Shoulder of Mutton		Westgate					1851
365	Shuttleworth's	36	George St to Kirkgate	1851	1872	1850		1851
366	Shuttleworth's		Westgate				1887	1823
367	Sidebottom's	87	Westgate	1881	1872	1852	1830	1823
368	Simpson's		Wonder St	1891			1904	
369	Slater's		Slater St	1881				
370	Smal(l) Page	9	Westmorland St	1851	1872	1850	1830	1851
371	Smith's		Westgate				1822	1851
372	Spawforth		Back Lane/Westgate	1851		1850	1887	1851
373	Spence's		Kirkgate			1850		
374	Spicer's		Kirkgate					1823
375	Spotted Leopard		Kirkgate		1872		1857	1851
376	Spread Eagle			1881				
377	Spurr	132-146	Stanley Rd	1881	1872		1887	
378	St John's Mill							
379	Stafford		Northgate	1851		1860	1847	
380	Stamp Office	13	Westgate to Rodney Yd	1881	1872		1862	1851
381	Star		Westgate			1850	1822	1823
382	Statter's		Kirkgate to Springs	1891	1915		1887	
383	Statter's		Providence St	1891	1915			
384	Stawman's		Providence St 1851					
385	Stead's		Kirkgate					1851
386	Stillings		Charles St	1851				
387	Stockdale		Kirkgate	1851	1872	1850	1857	1851
388	Stock's	67	Kirkgate	1851		1850	1857	
389	Stock's		Westgate				1830	
390	Stogden's		Kirkgate				1830	
391	Stonehouse's		Ings Rd	1881				
392	Stotter's Old		Kirkgate				1837	
393	Stott's		Westgate				1822	1823
394	Stafford		Bond Terrace				1857	

	Yard Name	No	Location	Census	YR.BK	Roll	Diry	Map
395	Stafford		Northgate			1850	1837	1851
396	Stafford Arms		Market Place				1853	
397	Strafforths						1862	
398	Stringer's		Westgate to Back Ln	1851		1869	1875	
399	Sun		Sun Lane	1851	1872			1851
400	Sunderland	246	Kirkgate to Ings Rd	1881	1872			1851
401	Swan		Westgate	1891	1915			
402	Swan With Two Necks	156	Westgate	1881			1857	
403	Sykes		Kirkgate	1881			1887	
404	T White's		Westgate					
405	Talbot		Westgate to Back Ln	1891	1915		1853	
406	Talbot & Falcon	40	Northgate	1851	1872	1850	1830	1823
407	Taylor		Stanley Rd	1881	1872		1887	
408	Taylor's	64	Kirkgate	1851	1872		1857	1823
409	Taylor's		Westgate	1881				
410	Theatre			1851	1875			
411	Thompson's	60	Westgate to Cliffe Parade	1851	1872	1850	1822	1823
412	Thornes Lane (Yd)		Thornes	1891				
413	Three Bells		Northgate					
414	Three Tuns	64	Northgate	1851	1872	1850		1823
415	Thresh's		Southgate	1891	1915			
416	Tidgewell		Westgate					
417	Tidswells		Back Lane/Westgate	1881		1850	1866	1851
418	Tofts		Northgate	1851	1872	1850	1842	
419	Top Gills			1881				
420	Trinity Church	144	Kirkgate				1892	
421	Tunnecliffe's		Kirkgate	1851				1851
422	Union		Kirkgate					
423	Vaudeville		Westgate		1915			
424	Volunteer	104	Kirkgate	1881	1872	1850	1837	1823
425	Wade's		Kirkgate	1851				
426	Wade's Mill		Thornes Lane Wharf				1904	
427	Wagon Warehouse		Westgate			1850		
428	Wainwright's		Kirkgate	1891			1887	
429	Walker	84-94	Stanley Rd	1891	1872		1853	
430	Waker's		Alverthorpe	1881				
431	Wallace		Ingwell St					
432	Walton's		Westgate				1830	
433	Ward's	c14	Commercial St	1891		1922		
434	Ward's		Market St/Albion Crt				1867	
435	Ward's		Providence St	1851				
436	Warehouse			1881				
437	Waterworks		Northgate	1891			1853	
438	Waterworks Office		Southgate					1851
439	Weaver Inn		Westgate					1823
440	Webb's		Bridge St	1851				
441	Webb and Yates		Bridge St	1851				
442	Webster	122	Stanley Rd	1891	1872	1887		
443	Webster's		Kirkgate	1851			1857	
444	Wellington		Wellington St, Batley Rd	1891			1922	
445	Wharf			1881				
446	Whittaker		Kirkgate					1823
447	White Hart		Westgate to Southgate	1851	1872	1850	1848	1823
448	White Horse	63	Westgate to Geo St	1851	1872	1850	1822	1823
449	White Swan		Kirkgate	1851				
450	White Swan	17	Westgate to Geo St	1851	1872	1850	1822	1823
451	White's		Westgate	1881	1872	1850	1834	1823
452	Widdop's			1891				
453	Wilby		Stanley Rd	1891				
454	Wilby's		Kirkgate			1850	1830	
455	Wild's	184	Kirkgate to Thornhill St	1851	1872	1850	1857	
456	Wild's	19	Thornes Lane				1927	
457	Wilson's		Northgate	1891	1915			
458	Wilson's		Park St		1915			
459	Wilson's		Providence St	1851				
460	Windmill	25	Westgate to Geo St	1851	1872	1850	1837	1823
461	Woodcock's		Kirkgate	1891				
462	Woodcock's		Northgate					
463	Wood's		Providence St	1851	1872		1887	1851
464	Woolpack's	54	Westgate	1851	1872	1850	1822	1823
465	Wright's			1881			1862	
466	Yard	154	Kirkgate				1861	
467	Yard	157	Kirkgate		1881		1861	
468	Yard	183	Kirkgate				1861	
469	Yard	57	Westgate				1861	
470	York Hotel	60	Westgate	1851			1922	

CONTRIBUTORS

1. CHEAPER BY THE YARD

Ann Barnes was born in Leeds, at 'Jimmy's', in 1944 but spent most of her childhood in Selby. She was educated at boarding school in the village Hillam, at Selby Girls' High School and at Wakefield School of Commerce. Her BSc degree, from the Open University, was obtained whilst she was not only working full time but also raising four sons.

Her essay on Bastardy in Ossett appeared in the first *Aspects of Wakefield.* She worked in the Local Studies Department, Balne Lane Library Headquarters for fifteen years before taking early retirement on medical grounds.

2. OSSETT GOLF CLUB 1909-1925

Brian Wallis was born in Middlestown, near Wakefield, and educated at Ossett Grammar School. He has a diploma in Industrial Management and his working life was spent at Slazenger/Dunlop Sports Co Ltd and with the Royal Mail.

Now retired, his interests lie in local history, genealogy, golf, snooker, travel and writing.

He is the author of *Echoes from an Old Fairway: A History of the Horbury and District Golf Club, 1907-1965, and Wakefield Golf Club Centenary 1891-1991.* He is a lifelong supporter of John Smith's Tadcaster Brewery.

3. THE BADSWORTH HUNT
9. HILLTOP, HILLSIDE AND RIVERSIDE
11. BREWING IN WAKEFIELD

John Goodchild is a native of Wakefield and was educated at the Grammar School there. He has been active in local historical research since about the age of thirteen, and is the author of over 140 books and published essays on aspects of the history of the Westt Riding. He was founder-curator of Cusworth Hall Museum and subsequently Archivisit to Wakefield MDC; in his retirement he runs a Local History Study Centre which houses his immense collection of manuscripts and research materials, and which is open to use, free of charge, by appointment. Mr Goodchild holds an honorary M Univ from the Open University, awarded for academic and scholarly distinction and for public services. He is a regular contributor to the Aspects Series. Outside historical research, his interests lie in Freemasonry and in Unitarinism - and his dog.

4. OF GRAVES AND EPITAPHS

Anthony Petyt was born in Wakefield and educated at Queen Elizabeth Grammar School. He then studied agriculture at Askham Bryan College, York and on qualifying joined the staff of the college farms. In 1964 he obtained a managerial post with a large farming company near Morley which held for the next seven years. In 1971 he decided to make a career change and became a residential social worker at the Henshaw's School for the Visually Handicapped at Harrogate. In 1974 he became a welfare officer with the Wakefield M D Council Education Department where he stayed until he took early retirement in 1996. He is the secretary of the

Gissing Trust and is involved with the running of the Gissing Centre in Thompson's Yard, Wakefield. Apart from Gissing research his interests include local history, genealogy and book collecting.

5. LEISURE IN VICTORIAN OSSETT

David Scriven moved to Yorkshire, where he now teaches history at Batley Grammar School, after studying at the Unviserty College of Wales, Aberystwyth. He has been interested in local history for more than twenty years and is a founder member of the Ossett Local History Society. He has carried out research on the social and economic development of Ossett in the nineteenth century and has given numerous talks on the subject as well as having an article published in *Old West Riding.*

6. THE STORY OF COOPER BROS

Derek Clayton has lived in the village of Thornes for seventy-six years. He was born in a house on Denby Dale Road and moved a year later to Thornes Road. He was educated at Christ Church Infants School and St James' Junior School, both in Thornes Lane, and later at Queen Elizabeth Grammar School. After working for a short time in the WRCC Education Department, he took a position with Wakefield Health Department, studying to become a sanitary inspector. Following two years' national service with the Reconnaissance Corps he qualified both as a sanitary inspector and a meat and food inspector. His career in local government continued with Dewsbury Corporation and the WRCC and ultimately he became Food Hygiene Officer for Barnsley MB Council, retiring in 1985. He has a lifelong interest in public transport, particularly buses, and is currently revising his history of the West Riding Automobile Company. He has written a history of

County Motors (Lepton) Ltd and is researching the east coast services of United Automobile Service Ltd.

7. THE ZIVILINTERNIERUNGSLAGER AT LOFTHOUSE PARK

Peter Wood was educated at Normanton Grammar School from 1944 to 1949 and served in the RAF before returning to work for a local engineering company. Later he went to Scawsby College of Education and then taught in Pontefract. He has been a member of Wakefield Historical Society and its council for over twenty years and became a vice-president three years ago. He has written and published a school history and the Sandal History Trail. He is currently involved in the preparation of a book covering Bell Vue, a district of Wakefield. He is involved with the U3A (University of Third Age) and walking groups and very interested in local history. He has taken part in study days for schools and archaeology open days at Sandal Castle and has undertaken enactments there. He is married with a son, and is a grandfather.

8. SOME MUTE INGLORIOUS MILTON

Edward Green was brought up in Wrenthorpe and educated at Outwood Grange Comprehensive School. A former chorister with Wakefield Cathedral Choir, he studied economics at Portsmouth University graduating in 1990. His keen interest in history and concern over vanishing local heritage led him to write and publish his book *Wrenthorpe: A History in 1992.* Edward is currently working for a Research Agency and is about to complete an MA in history for which he has been studying part time. In 1999 Edward launched an internet web site dedicated to the history of Wrenthorpe. Other interests include nature conservation, playing the violin and restoring and maintaining a classic car.

---

10. YOUNG WOMEN AT WORK IN OSSETT

After completing a degree in history and librarianship at the University College of Wales, Aberystwyth, **Deborah Scriven** married and moved to Yorkshire. She has worked in a number of public libraries in the district and is currently Local Studies Librarian at Wakefield Library Headquarters. She is a founder member of Ossett and District Historical Society and is a member of the Council of Wakefield Historical Society. Her article on young women at work in Ossett is a revised version of a project completed for the Open University course, 'Studying Family and Community History', (DA301).

---

12. THE ENCOURAGEMENT OF KINDLY INTERCOURSE

Coral 'Kate' Taylor was born in Wakefield in 1933 and educated at the Girls' High School before going on to St Anne's College, Oxford, where she read English Language and Literature. After teaching in Leeds, at West Park CS School and the City Leeds and Carnegie College, she took up a post as Principal Lecturer in English at Wentworth Castle College of Education at Stainborough. Following the closure of the college she became Vice-Principal (Community) at Barnsley Sixth Form College when it opened in 1979. Since her retirement in 1990 she has spent time researching local history, in the fields of leisure and entertainment. She is Hon Managing Editor of Wakefield Historical Publications and the Chair of Mercia Cinema Society.

INDEX OF PEOPLE